Ruth Prawer Jhabvala's Novels

Woman amidst Snares and Delusions

Rishi Pal Singh

Published by
ATLANTIC
PUBLISHERS & DISTRIBUTORS (P) LTD
7/22, Ansari Road, Darya Ganj,
New Delhi-110002
Phones : +91-11-40775252, 23273880, 23275880, 23280451
Fax : +91-11-23285873
Web : www.atlanticbooks.com
E-mail : info@atlanticbooks.com

Branch Office
5, Nallathambi Street, Wallajah Road,
Chennai-600002
Phones : +91-44-64611085, 32413319
E-mail : chennai@atlanticbooks.com

ISBN 978-81-269-1277-3

Printed in India at Nice Printing Press, A-33/3A, Site-IV, Industrial Area, Sahibabad, Ghaziabad, U.P.

Dedicated to

My affectionate sister
SUMAN
—a flower—who withered in
her spring and left for her
heavenly abode on 19 June 1986

Preface

An exposition of the feminine sensibility in the creative works of a woman writer and from a woman's point of view is really an enchanting phenomenon for a student of literature. My motivation in selecting Ruth Prawer Jhabvala for an analytical and comprehensive study of the feminine sensibilities in her novels has been the result of the same curiosity about this fictionist who has articulated the whole gamut of feminine feelings and passions, hopes and aspirations, and fears and frustrations of the womenfolk of at least three prominent continents of this planet. This European woman remained transplanted in India and then moved to the United States for a wider exposure to her literary genius in the cosmopolitan cultural confluence. This fortuitously 'ever exiled' status has given a triangular mode to her literary sensibility and artistic craftsmanship. With a self-avowed chameleon changeability and ironic vision of a social realist, Jhabvala has portrayed the predicament of the feminine sensibilities ranging from the tabooed Indian women and illusionary European women in Indian milieu to the enigmatic and self-destructive women of American emigre community.

Ruth Prawer Jhabvala occupies a conspicuous position as a fictionist in the contemporary literary scenario, and as an explorer of the deep recesses of feminine soul and psyche she is second to none of her sex.

Apart from some fascinating short stories and screenplays, Jhabvala has written twelve novels so far and the central figures in her works are women on a persistent quest for self-identity and individuality. In the first five novels Jhabvala has depicted the traditional life of the Indian women with all the taboos, inhibitions, oppressions, filth and squalor at large. The predicament of the illusionary European women facing a doom in Indian milieu has been articulated in her novels of the second literary phase. In the novels of third phase her literary vision has widened to acquire the cosmopolitan dimension as she articulates the self-delusive and self-destructive inner fragmentation, psychic disorder, boredom and abnormal sexuality.

No doubt, Ruth Prawer Jhabvala has recently gained a rapid popularity among the readers as well as the critical analysts of literature in India and some remarkable research works have been done on her fiction. R.S. Singh has explored the theme of European reaction to the typical Indian milieu. The question of Ruth Jhabvala's western identity has been well presented by S. Krishnaswamy in his research *White Woman's Burden*. Kavita A. Sharma has studied the theme of spiritualism in *Jhabvala on Godman*. Meenakshi Mukherjee in *Explorations in Modern Indo-English Fiction* has thrown light on Jhabvala's passage to India under the title *Journey's End for Jhabvala*. The aspect of East-West encounter has been much ploughed with almost identical conclusions. But so far no exclusive research work has been attempted to explore the mysterious predicament of the feminine sensibility in the novels of Ruth Prawer Jhabvala. I have felt it imperative to explore this prominent aspect of her creative works for a judicious and worthy appraisal of her novels. Her wide humanity, her superb theme of feminine sensibilities and woman's search for self-definition and self-actualisation is an excellent aspect of her novels and its analytical survey will undoubtedly give an innovative interpretation to her literature. In a nutshell, my work is an honest attempt to explore this theme and I have a glowing faith that my research will open new vistas for a just and wise comprehension of Jhabvala's novels.

The title of the work itself defines the scope and purpose of my study. The work is divided into six chapters—1. Introduction, 2. Cultural Backgrounds *vis-à-vis* Feminine Sensibility, 3. Early Phase: The Indian Women, 4. Middle Phase: The Western Women in Love with India and Indians, 5. Final Phase: Women in the Cross-cultural Amalgam of the American Milieu, and 6. Summing-Up. The first chapter presents a brief sketch of the life of Ruth Prawer Jhabvala and also her making up as a literary artist. In the same chapter I have also attempted to define the title feminine sensibility in the traditional as well as the modern perspectives of the term. The four core chapters 2, 3, 4 and 5 are self-explanatory of the matter discussed in them. I have explored here the various aspects of the feminine sensibilities as articulated by the novelist progressively in her novels. Chapter 6 is an attempt to summarize the findings of this study to assess this novelist's contribution to the fictional world and humanity in the light of the subject. Bibliography has been given at the end of book so as to facilitate further reading of the students. The textual quotations are marked with abbreviated form of novels for the purpose of convenience but they are strictly adhered to the publications referred in footnotes and Bibliography.

This preface will remain incomplete if I fail to acknowledge my indebtedness to those scholars, friends, relatives and literary agencies that extended every possible help during my study and writing this book. I will always remain indebted to my two old friends to whom my gratitude will best be expressed by leaving them unnamed.

I am obliged to many critics acknowledged and many more who have remained unacknowledged whose ideas helped me immensely in forming views expressed in the work. I am also grateful to the librarian and staff of British Council Library New Delhi, Sahitya Akademi Library New Delhi, Delhi University Library Delhi, Central Library Calcutta, Jiwaji University Gwalior, M.L.B. (Autonomous) College Gwalior and Aligarh Muslim University Aligarh. I am equally thankful to Mr. Sonu, the owner of 'Likhar Computers' who painstakingly typed my thesis.

I must also acknowledge my gratefulness to my wife Kalpana Gurjar without whose patience and persistent cooperation this work would have been merely a dream. I feel pleasure in expressing my special thanks and love to my curious son master Aayush and daughter baby Mudita who rigorously imbued me with a zeal needed to complete this work. I will be failing in my sincerity if I do not acknowledge my indebtedness to my reverent father Ch. Hukum Singh and love pouring mother Smt. Narayani Devi, whose blessings and idealism have always been great inspiring force in my life. Above all, I acknowledge my heartfelt thankfulness to the Almighty for steering me out of all hurdles and problems in the pursuit of this work.

Rishi Pal Singh

Contents

1
Introduction

Ruth Prawer Jhabvala, a world class fictionist and storyteller of the present century, has distinctive achievements as a literary artist. Jhabvala's creativity as a feminine writer is the result of her European sensibility modified, enriched and also enraged by her Indian family life and twenty-five years' stay in this country and then her flight to America for a greater exposure to her genius there. This passage from Europe to India and from here to the United States has given a triangular mode to her thematic perceptions and literary craftsmanship. Ruth Jhabvala has cultivated and demonstrated the literary qualities which are peculiarly her own and which primarily emerge from the comprehensive portrayal of the various modes of feminine sensibility along with her artistic vision widening from phase to phase of her career.

Ruth Prawer Jhabvala's fiction centres around women as she explicates the issues that feminism grapples with and there are no memorable male characters in her works. It is quintessentially Jhabvala's thematic dimension that always deals with womanhood in various settings encompassing three continents. Exuberant and morbid, sly and compassionate, mysterious and explicit the fiction of Jhabvala has enchanted the readers whom she by 1975 expected to be British; even her North American audience while somewhat newer is no less enthusiastic. She has been called a truly genius author with immense literary achievements, and her oeuvre subtle and magnificent while India is a marvellous whetstone for her sharp humanity and retractable claws. We observe a live portrayal of the feminine quest for identity and self-actualisation in the dominating traditionalism of Indian society on the one hand and the obsessive self-delusion and self-destruction of women in the cosmopolitan set up of modern western world on the other.

Proverbially speaking an artist is born, not made. However, all beings imbibe traits and trends from a number of phenomena; one quite significant of these is the rearing up of a person. It has been well said that a child's first school is the family wherein he/she gets the first lesson between the kisses of mother and caresses of father. All persons have some inborn inherited qualities and some qualities that they pick up in the company of persons they interact with. Thus, it will be in the fitness of things to have a bird's eye-view of Ruth Prawer Jhabvala's life-sketch and various shaping influences on her as a person and as a literary artist.

Ruth Prawer Jhabvala's presence in the present literary scenario, poses an intriguing problem of her authorial classification and by now so many readers are familiar with the outline of her unusual biography which has imparted far-reaching influences to her fictional world. Ruth Prawer was born in Cologne on 7 May 1927, into what was, on her mother's side, a well-established German-Jewish family: Eleonora Cohn married the lawyer Marcus Prawer, a Polish Jew recently arrived in Germany; like many others he fled enforced conscription in the First World War. In the Second World War, the immediate family—Ruth Prawer's parents and one brother—only narrowly escaped the catastrophic fate of most European Jews, sailing to England as late as April 1939. But most of the others—her father's entire family, part of her mother's family, the children she first went to school with and most of her parents' family friends were lost.

The four Prawers came to England as displaced persons among those lucky refugees allowed to live anywhere. She received her education at Hindon County School, London and later at Queen Mary College, University of London. She studied English Literature earning an M.A. degree in 1951 and her thesis *The Short Story in England 1700-1750* was a nice hint at her future career as a master storyteller. Thus, the talented children survived and prospered—Ruth Prawer's brother Seigbart Prawer became a professor of German literature at Oxford and an established author—but Marcus Prawer committed suicide in London in the fifties. With such disastrous losses and upheavals in her early childhood, Ruth Prawer had already started writing fiction in German. After completing her university education she negotiated the switch to English and soon her drawers were stuffed with unfinished plays, stories and novels—an evidence that writing came to her as naturally as breathing.

Ruth Prawer met and then married C.S.H. Jhabvala an Indian student of architecture. With him she moved to India in 1951 and here she remained for a substantial period of two and a half decades of family life. Their three daughters grew up in Delhi, the city of the author's fortuitous settlement in India. In India R. Prawer Jhabvala, as she somewhat cryptically signed herself, became a writer with worldwide recognition. Eight out of her twelve novels as well as five collections of short stories were written and set in India, published in England and United States and also intended for a western reader. Jhabvala, though originally a European, felt Indian milieu on her pulse and her novels of Indian setting are fictional expressions of her observation of the socio-cultural predicament of women whether they are indigenous Indians or the expatriate Europeans.

Another major turn in Ruth Prawer Jhabvala's literary career came in 1975, when she left this country of her family life and settled in New York. With this turning point Jhabvala's biography literalised her outsiderhood, the outsiderhood of this already exiled European author who remained always on move with her position of a permanent refugee.[1] Now, a new international dimension of her fiction having cosmopolitan characters in the émigré community of America is picturised but still mixed with the reminiscence of her passage through this obsessive country which has wrought indelible influences on her sensibility. There her reputation among the American audience was heightened with the 1983 award to her of the Mac Arthur Foundation's prestigious 'genius' grant. Though it is as a writer of fiction that Jhabvala has earned the highest praise, her simultaneous career in America as a screen writer in steady collaboration with the director James Ivory and producer Ismail Merchant has brought about an equal recognition to her. Besides some enchanting short stories Ruth Prawer Jhabvala has written twelve novels which are: *Amrita: To Whom She Will* (1955), *The Nature of Passion* (1956), *Esmond in India* (1957), *The Householder* (1960), *Get Ready for Battle* (1962), *A Backward Place* (1965), *A New Dominion* (1972), *Heat and Dust* (1975), *In Search of Love and Beauty* (1983), *Three Continents* (1987), *Poet and Dancer* (1993) and *Shards of Memory* (1995). Nevertheless, the portrayal of the predicament of the feminine sensibilities in varying degrees has been the main theme of all of Ruth Jhabvala's literary pursuits, which project her women protagonists in distinct backgrounds.

One of the most puzzling phenomena of the literary world is the intriguing problem of Ruth Prawer Jhabvala's identity and classification as an artist and various views have been expressed on this issue. Highlighting the importance of this problem in relation to Jhabvala, David Rubin writes:

> The solution to this puzzle of national identification is not idly speculative for on it hangs the far more complex mystery of Jhabvala's sense of her own identity and its relation to the world she has created and ultimately of the real value and meaning of her fiction.[2]

A group of biographers argues that Ruth Jhabvala is a 'Jewish' writer and a study of her creative works could not be complete without Jewish implications. They also correlate the refugee wanderer women protagonists of her novels to that of the author's own rootless life full of traumatic events and exiles. But to argue that Jhabvala is a Jewish writer runs considerable risks.[3] In the first case there exists the alarming possibility that one's intentions might be misunderstood or misinterpreted. Because of a long history of anti-semitism, to attempt to attach the label of 'Jew' might be seen as a kind of provocation, different from attaching any neutral national label such as 'Pole' or 'Swiss' or any religious or denominational label such as 'Protestant' or 'Anglican'. To insist on specifically 'Jewish' qualities or attributes in individuals who consider themselves either German or English or some other nationality has an unfortunate precedence among anti-semitics who discovered that—*Once a Jew, always a Jew*—slogan served their various nefarious designs. Jhabvala is totally different from the definition of a Jew in strict code of originality.

The most authentic explanations about her national and literary identity are the frequent statements made by Ruth Jhabvala herself in her many interviews and non-fictional essays full of autobiographical commentary. In her non-fictional essay *Myself in India*[4], Ruth Prawer Jhabvala refers to herself most frequently as 'European' or some variant of this. But just as frequently she refers to herself as an 'exile' having no country to which she really belongs. "I was practically born a displaced person," she has said, "and all any of us ever wanted was a travel document and a residential permit."[5] Thus, Jhabvala is, though displaced yet totally different from the definition of a Jew in strict code of originality. Even beyond this she declared in 1991:

> I can trace no influence of my Jewish background in myself or my writing. I seem to have grown not out of my own but other people's roots, whether Indian or European or Anglo-Saxon,... I know this doesn't sound very plausible, and is probably due to my not looking far or deep, but there it is:[6]

Despite her statements expressing her need to disavow her past, it will be more profitable to pursue any study of the author's oeuvre with an eye on her past to grasp the value of present creativity. This condition of permanent exile, something she does repeatedly acknowledge, is after all a direct consequence of her past identity and of her origin. When her essay *Myself in India* is examined in detail it reveals not just the westerner's ordinary struggle with India but a complex person's extraordinary struggle in this mysteriously obsessive land. Ronald Shepherd, after an analytical study of this non-fictional document of Jhabvala, has commented: "Exiled and rootless, this is a personality which craves for external support, needs to tap into other people's roots in order to proffer an adequate face and identity."[7]

Therefore, Ruth Jhabvala's 'English-made' European identify must be seen in the context of a self-avowed chameleon changeability in India. Her relationship with India is an extraordinarily tangled one because she remained committed to India in a way and for a length of time unusual among the gamut of western writers who have taken India as their subject. Here it will be very useful to see what Jhabvala herself has said about her identity as a European writer in India:

> The central fact for all my work, as I see it, is that I am a European living permanently in India. I've lived here for most of my adult life and have an Indian family. This makes me not quite an insider but it does not leave me entirely an outsider either. I feel my position to be at a point in space where I have quite a good view of both sides but am myself left stranded in the middle. My work is an attempt to charter this unchartered territory for myself.... My books may appear to be objective but really I think they are the opposite: for I describe the Indian scene not for its own sake but for mine.... My work is only one individual European's attempt to compound the puzzling process of living in India.[8]

This straightforward and candid statement made in 1972 offers valuable clues that Jhabvala remained a detached observer in her fiction dealing with India and Indians.[9] Not only this she also expected her reader to be a westerner only as she did proclaim: "When one writes about India as European and in English, as I do, inevitably one writes not for Indian but for western reader."[10]

Pursuing Jhabvala's description of herself a little further in the country of her exile, we must be cautiously mindful. In *Myself in India*, Jhabvala has pointed out the paradoxical and ambivalent nature of the westerners' response to India. She describes a process, which starts in cycles-starting with love, turning to hate and working through to become love once again and she tells of the countless cycles she has passed through. As the essay proceeds it is India and Indians who are named and a division of author's single narrative voice into several antagonistic voices becomes apparent.

Due to all these confessional expressions of the author so many Indian scholars have charged her of detachment and inability to understand the deep realities of India.[11] They argue that, in spite of her marriage and long passage through India, Jhabvala could never become a genuine Indian voice just as Kamala Markandaya (married to an Englishman and living permanently in London) could not become a British. So many Indian readers and critics have attacked the self-avowed rootlessness of this expatriate European who entered in Indian family life by her fortuitous marriage with a Parsi and here we must realise that the Parsis-Persians are themselves of an outsider group in India.[12] Very much like the Jews in their diaspora, they value education, actively pursue professional status and retain a somewhat separate identity. Perhaps, this aloofness of her husband's community in India is also to some extent responsible for her limited experience in India—the primitive country of her ambivalent indictment.

Always on a move and on a permanent exile, Jhabvala's final move to New York provided a new dimension to her personality and literary talent. Her exposure to the cosmopolitan culture of America and its émigré community enriched her sensibility to deal with the international labyrinth of human relationships from a feminine point of view. With this turning point Jhabvala's biography literalised her outsiderhood, and all the scholarly deliberations and speculations classifying her an authentic Indian author have proved insufficient. Khushwant Singh's attempt to cite Jhabvala along with R.K. Narayan in 1961 as one of the two best novelists of India writing in English now sounds as an unreliable and unsustainable assessment of this expatriate daughter-in-law of India.[13] But she is always a refugee on move on the international arena of experiences, commercialism and literary craftsmanship. Now Ruth Jhabvala like V.S. Naipaul has become an international writer dealing with the variously displaced and misplaced persons—most of them of mixed race, mixed culture and mixed sexuality. Moreover, now her focus has reached deep into the subconscious and unconscious of these women characters and she explores the enigma of self-delusive and self-destructive illusions, anxiety, psychic malaise and ennui in rootless society with a magical ability and the feminine point of view.

NOTES

1. V.A. Shahane, "An Artist's Experience of India: Jhabvala's Fiction", *Commonwealth Fiction*, ed. R.K. Dhawan (New Delhi: Classical Publishing Company, 1988), p. 228.
2. David Rubin, Ruth Jhabvala in India, in Modern Fiction Studies; 30th Anniversary Issue, *Winter*, Vol. 30, No. 4, 1984, p. 672.
3. Ronald Shepherd, "A Question of Identity: The Non-fiction", *Ruth Prawer Jhabvala in India*: *The Jewish Connection* (New Delhi: Chanakya Publication, 1994), p. 9.
4. Ruth Prawer Jhabvala, *Myself in India*: *An Experience of India*, John Murray, 1971, pp. 7-20.
5. Quoted in Ronald Shepherd, *op. cit.*, p. 9.
6. Ruth Prawer Jhabvala's Personal Letter (May 13, 1991) quoted in Ronald Shepherd's *A Question of Identity*, *op. cit.*, p. 10.
7. Ronald Shepherd, *op. cit.*, p. 11.
8. Ruth Prawer Jhabvala, quoted in *Contemporary Novelists* (New York: St. Martin's Press, 1976), p. 270.
9. Nissim Ezekiel, "Distorting Mirror; Review of *Heat and Dust*", *The Times of India*, 4 January 1976, p. 10.
10. Jhabvala, "Moonlight, Jasmine and Rickets", *The New York Times* (New York, April 22, 1975), p. 55.
11. C. Paul Verghese, "A Note on Esmond in India", *Journal of India Writing in English*, July (1976), pp. 33-37.
12. Meenakshi Mukherjee, "The Ruthless Jhabvala Touch: Review of How I Became a Holy Mother", *The Times of India*, 12 Sept., 1976, p. 10.
13. Khushwant Singh, "The Literary Scene", *International Literary Annual*, III (London, 1961), p. 174.

2

Cultural Backgrounds *vis-à-vis* Feminine Sensibility

Before dwelling upon this central theme in the novels of Ruth Prawer Jhabvala it is equally imperative to discuss the feminine sensibility and development of feminism in creative literature especially fiction. In this regard since antiquity it has been taken for granted that the reader, writer and even critic of literature is male and it assumes the exclusion of female voice from the institution of literature obviously shunning her as an inferior sex. The deliberation on feminism in literary context, particularly in the recent fiction and from a woman's point of view, is an endeavour of a highly innovative nature representing a significant departure from the traditional mode of social decorum and prudish notions in the male-dominated world. The articulation of the whole gamut of the feminine feelings and passions, hopes and aspirations and fears and traumas through women protagonists and by women writers is a phenomenon of new development in literature. The feminist writers, especially women, have forged a fictional strategy to project the core recesses of women from a woman's point of view in accordance with the pressures and challenges to which they have been subjected. This new approach offers a new innovative perspective of literature and emphasizes the need for a search of new paradigms in the age-old dominance of male views in the world of letters.

To have a clear understanding of the issue of feminine sensibility, it is also essential to distinguish between 'feminism', 'feminine', and 'female'. These three terms have been used in multitudinous ways. Toril Moi defines 'feminism' as a political position, 'femaleness' as a matter of biology and 'femininity' as a sort of culturally determined characteristics. She says that the words 'feminism' and 'feminist' are political labels supporting the aims of women's movement of the 1960's. In her phenomenal study *Sexual/Textual Politics* (1969) she observes that the essence of politics is power and the task of feminist critics and theorists is to expose the ways of male dominance over females.[1] Simon de Beauvoir, the French writer, wrote *The Second Sex* (1949-50) under the influence of Sartre's phallocentric categories.[2]

An important precursor of feminist criticism was Virginia Woolf who in addition to her fiction wrote numerous lectures and essays on women authors and on cultural, economic and educational disabilities within what she called a Patriarchal society that have hindered or prevented women from realizing their creative possibilities.[3] It is true that when in 1928 Virginia Woolf delivered a modest lecture called "A Room of One's Own" nobody could have foreseen that one day it would give rise to a new thinking on issues pertaining to the status and role of women. Rosalind Coward discussing the existing confusion of 'feminist' with 'female' in her essay *Are Women's Novels Feminist Novels?* writes that it is just not possible to say that women-centered writings have any necessary relationship to feminism.[4]

Therefore, it is a misconception that the very act of describing experience typical of a woman's life is a feminist act. Now the question arises if feminists do not have to write exclusively on female writers then man too can be feminist. To this Toril Moi says: "Yes men can be feminist—but they can't be women, just as whites can be anti-racist but not black. Under patriarchy men will always speak from a different position than women."[5]

The confusion of 'feminine' with 'female' ultimately leads to essentialism. The terms 'feminine' and 'masculine' represent social constructs—patterns of sexuality and behaviour imposed by cultural and social norms. In this usage feminine represents 'nurture' and female 'nature'. Femininity is thus a social construct. As Simon de Beauvoir says "One isn't born a woman but rather becomes a woman: It is civilization as a whole that produces this creature which is described as feminine."[6] Patriarchal oppression imposes certain social standards of femininity on all biological women in order to prove that these standards for femininity are natural. T.N. Singh observes:

> Notwithstanding all this, the general notion about woman as a shadow figure to a male care taker, be he a father, a husband or a son continues to persist. The situation calls for a concerted effort to demolish such notions and to affirm the dignity of woman in the family as well as in the wider social life.[7]

To make women believe that there is such a thing as essence of femaleness called femininity serves the interests of patriarchy. Conscious of the evils originating from patriarchy modern women would not endorse the wisdom of Tennysonian demarcation between man and woman in *The Princess, V* (1847):

> Man for the field and woman for the hearth;
> Man for the sword and for the needle she:
> Man to command and woman to obey.
> All else confusion.[8]

This might have suited the Victorian age of compromise and priggishness—the age which did not think it proper to grant franchise and equality to womankind but modern times will hardly approve it. While books like Simon de Beauvoir's *The Second Sex* nurtured the feminist ideology, it was in the seventies and eighties of the last century that various issues touching women were considered systematically. A positive sense of feminine identity has found recognition now and women are stepping out of the rigid sex roles assigned to them traditionally. In the western world and the urban patches of India they are busy with 'self-actualising' having identities not dependent on men. To the Victorian attitude of Tennyson a pet reply comes from the Indian poetess Kamala Das who rebelliously proclaims that:

> I shall someday leave, leave the cocoon,
> You build around me with morning tea,
> Love-words flung from door ways and of course
> Your tired lust, I shall someday take
> Wings, fly around....[9]

Robin Morgan also wrote in words glowing with resentment, pity and humanism:

> There is something every woman bears around her neck on a thin chain of fear—an amulet of madness. For each of us, there exists somewhere a moment of insult so intense that she will reach up and rip the amulet off even if the chain tears at the flesh of her neck.... We are rising: powerful in our unclean bodies: bright glowing mad in our inferior brains: wild hair flying, wild eyes staring, wild voices keening; stuffing fingers into our mouth to stop the screams of fear and hate and pity for men we have loved and love still.[10]

These words, fierce both in hatred and in love, express the depth, complexity and multiplicity of feminism. Perhaps, it can be said that there is no feminism; there are feminisms ranging from the purely rebellious stance of the shrieking, bra-burning type to the more balanced multivalent 'womanist' and humanist and even committed to survival and wholeness of entire people—male and female. No woman or man either can walk safe upon her or his own shadow and any brand of feminism which denies the woman's essential brand of femininity, thereby making her an Amazonian oddity is as much of an aberration as an effeminate male.

The problem still remains to define femininity. Under patriarchy a whole series of feminine characteristics such as sweetness, modesty, subservience, humility, etc. have been developed. If feminists try to develop another set of feminine virtues it would just become a part of the metaphysical binary oppositions. The French-Bulgarian psychoanalyst Julia Kristeva's consideration of femininity as marginality offers a position and not a definition. In Kristeva's terms femininity is simply that which is marginalized by the patriarchal symbolic order. This consideration of femininity in rational perspective is as shifting as the various forms of patriarchy itself. Kristeva's emphasis on marginality allows the repression of feminine as a position and not the essence.

The positional perspective on the meaning of feminity can be used to avoid the dangers of biologism: but then in deconstructing female out of experience, the very foundation of feminist struggle will disappear. Kristeva in her article "Women's Time"[11] advocates a deconstructive approach to sexual difference and argues for feminist struggle to be seen historically and politically as a three-tier phenomenon:

(a) Women demand equal access to the symbolic order considered—Liberal feminism—equality.

(b) Women reject the male symbolic order in the name of difference termed—Radical feminism—femininity extolled.

(c) Women reject the dichotomy between masculine and feminine as metaphysical—challenge to the very notion of separate entity.

However, it is essential to defend woman as woman in order to counteract the patriarchal order that despises woman as woman. Chaman Nahal's own concept of feminism is as:

> I define feminism as a mode of existence in which the woman is free of the dependence syndrome. There is a dependence syndrome: Whether it is the husband or the father or the community or whether it is a religious group, ethnic group. When women free themselves of the dependence syndrome and lead a normal life, my idea of feminism materializes.[12]

We have to aim at a society in which we have ceased to categorise logic, conceptualization and rationality as 'masculine' and not for one from which these virtues have been expelled as 'unfeminine'. Feminine sensibility comes out at its best in the writings of procreative women gifted with a fertile imagination. Such women writers are very convincing when they articulate about purely feminine sensibilities, which are sustained by love of man since love renders the vision clear, freeing it from all distortions and passions.

Though awakening of the female writers to a sense of their own identity began at the turn of the twentieth century projecting the woman struggling for individuality and self-realization, the modern women writers are much more vociferous in raising the issues of womanhood in the male-dominated surrounding. Love, sex and marriage are surely the primary needs of the human race but motherhood, child-bearing and child-rearing are the prerogatives of the womankind and the sense of fulfillment, contentment, and self-realisation comes to her through these natural processes. Procreation constitutes the core of love and sex between males and females: it forms the basis of a happy family and society at large. Women writers treat these themes with a sense of ease and confidence and their only self-agonising cry is against what man has made of woman.

Before coming to examine the presentation of the feminine problems by Ruth Prawer Jhabvala, a brief survey of how women writers have explored the problems of womanhood through fiction has also to be taken into consideration. It was about two hundred years back when Jane Austen, as a writer, had a sensitive awareness of the constraints and handicaps of her sex. This may be said of other women writers of the nineteenth century as well. Social decorum and prudish notions of morality proved in their case tyrannically inhibiting factors. Man could very well ignore them but for a woman a defiant attitude towards these rigid norms could not but have disastrous consequences. A woman writer had to restrict herself only to certain permissible areas of life and many domains of human experience remained forbidden to her.

Social environment has radically changed in Europe since then and the women writers enjoy a greater measure of freedom now. Feminine talent has found a full-throated expression and no area of life remains the exclusive male preserve any more. Women writers have endeavoured to demolish the idol-image of woman as a mere sex object and they have attempted a new definition of womanhood and woman's role in wider frame of human society. This was initiated by Virginia Woolf in 1928 by giving a clear and confessional exposure to the feelings, sentiments, and aspirations passing through woman's consciousness. Her writing justified itself by bringing about a radical transformation in public attitude towards man-woman relationship. In English fiction itself, we read a good number of feminine texts partly to have vicarious pleasure, partly to see how women feel. Katherine Anne Porter in a review of *Lady Chatterley's Lover* questioned how Lawrence could write about the sexual feelings of a woman. Her argument was that he is only a man.[13] If we follow this argument, then one has to be a hermaphrodite to write a novel at least about women.

In contemporary world of writers in English fiction there are numerous women novelists portraying the feminine soul and psyche through stream of consciousness technique in bold and defiant ways. In French feminists Simon de Beauvoir and others are very much concerned about the physical suppression of women. Therefore, according to the French model of feminism, it would imply the greater sexual expression. If we consider the American models, they are vociferous and most outspoken about the most inner feelings, emotions, desires and aspirations of womankind. As regards India, a brief note will reveal how well feminism has been presented and how replaced models are possible within the Indian context. The first generations of Indian writing in English have dealt with many problems of India but unfortunately have not touched the inner self of women folk.[14]

Let us now consider the Indian women writers of fiction in English who have depicted the feminine sufferings and defiant upsurges under the socio-cultural stresses and strains in traditional and conservative Indian setup. One such example is Nayantara Sahgal all of whose novels talk about women who are oppressed by marriage, by political circumstances, by accidents of history. These women characters attempt to break out of that shell of confinement in this male-dominated world. *A Time To Be Happy*, *This Time of Morning*, *The Day in Shadow*, *A Situation in Delhi*, *Rich Like Us*, are good feminist novels. Then we must refer to those Indian writers who have tried to hit back with whatever force they have. One such writer is Raji Narasimhan whose novel *Forever Free* (1979) is a very good example of establishing a different feminine model of living through defiance. The principal character—the woman called Shree, undergoes discord in marriage. Her husband has strange ways of looking at things for which she is not responsible at all, e.g. one of her husband's beliefs is that if the second toe is larger than the main toe, then the woman is surely adulterous. She is condemned right away without even being given any chance to be tried. What does a woman do in such a situation? There is no choice but to hit back and that is what the girl does in the novel.

Uma Vasudev is another novelist whose novel *The Song for Anusuiya* (1978) is an arrogant repercussion of ill-treatment of woman by man. Here the protagonist pays back to the men in their own coins. Anusuiya uses men and discards them. And why not? If a man can do this, why can't a woman? Uma Vasudev's novel is a good illustration of a woman who uses men as she wants to and is happy with herself. After all the whole aim of living of any human being and so of woman also, is to develop his/her personality to its optimum potentiality. Attia Hossain is another woman novelist who has used the metaphor of locked up confinement of woman in her novel *Sunlight on a Broken Column* (1961).

Another group of Kamala Markandaya, Anita Desai and Shashi Deshpande is that of prose-rhapsodists specialized in depicting the feelings, sentiments and emotions of womankind with a further progressive stride. Kamala Markandaya's novel *Nectar in a Sieve* (1954) is a fine illustration of change through conformity. Rukmani in the novel accepts everything. Whether it is Nathan's adultery or Ira's prostitution, all misfortunes are accepted by her.[15] However, it is difficult to explain why in Markandaya's novels there has to be a white man to aid her women characters. Anita Desai and Shashi Deshpande have a mastery in articulating the undulations of the female ego or self under the pressure of critical human situations and emotional relationships. The element of tiredness, boredom, disgust, bitterness, male-female rivalry and the feminist upsurge of ego are focused with an ironic vision by these feminine fictionists of great importance.[16]

Shashi Deshpande's novel *That Long Silence* makes the revelation of various discordant notes that meet and unite in the complex nature of Jaya who is a model of patience, endurance, devotion, integrity, rebellion, defiance and disobedience at the same time. She is all along pursuing the idea of self-knowledge and a separate identity. Jaya's dam of long silence and tolerance is broken and the result is a flood of egotistical assertions and emotional explosion.

What was just an emerging phenomenon of women's problems in the writings of female novelists like Anita Desai, has assumed a strident posture in Shobha De and other new signatures in the Indian fiction in English. Shobha De's popular novels *Socialite Evenings* (1988), *Starry Nights* (1990), *Sisters* (1992), *Strange Obsession* (1992) and *Snapshots* (1995) indicate the arrival of a new Indian woman eager to defy rebelliously the well-entrenched moral orthodoxy of the patriarchal social system. Through her novels Shobha De has tried to shatter patriarchal hegemony of this primitive social system. Woman's significant difference underlines her sexuality and it is from her sexuality that most of the problems arise. In fact, De's novels seem to be the modern version of the picaresque novels of the eighteenth century but the picaro in this case is woman and she too is avid for experiences.[17] In her novels woman, therefore, is most defiant and proclaims her independence and new self-definition. De opines that all people need sex and it is something special, something beautiful, something shared but the woman would get sex on her own terms now. The very fact, she adds, "that sex is no longer the most dreadful and despised three-letter word in India, is enough cause to celebrate".[18] But there is nothing derogatory or clandestine in sex. In fact, sex is the bedrock of all relationships. So the women in Shobha De's novels have broken all the sexual taboos with gusto and they discuss and practise sex with unusual candour. De also tears to pieces all the notions of respectability associated with marriage. Her interviews reveal that "Indian men make the world's lousiest lovers. They are high on ego, low on performance."[19] The modern feminists may learn a lesson or two from Shobha De or her women characters. Frailty's name is no longer woman; given a chance she can easily become woe-man.

Ruth Prawer Jhabvala, as it is to be justified by this research work, occupies a conspicuous position as a fictionist of well-defined feminine sensibility in the contemporary literary scenario and may be compared with the best of women writers of the day. It would be no exaggeration to state that in point of popularity as an explorer of feminine feelings, passions, hopes and fears she is second to none of her sex. Her European sensibility, transplanted in India and after experiencing Indian essence of feminine life her final exposition in America has given a triangular mode to her perception and articulation of feminine soul and psyche. Her wide humanity, her superb theme of 'search for self definition of woman': ranging from tabooed Indian women and European expatriate women in India to the enigmatic and essenceless life of American women make Jhabvala stand apart from many novelists of English language.

The exploration of these thematic phenomena of the feminine sensibility widening progressively along with artistic vision of this author will certainly open new vistas for a judicious and worthy comprehension of Jhabvala's literary world and craftsmanship as a fictionist of excellence.

NOTES

1. Toril Moi, "Sexual/Textual Politics", quoted in *Points of View*, Vol. 11, No. 2, Winter 1995, p. 3.
2. Simon de Beauvoir, "The Second Sex" (1949-50) quoted in *Points of View*, Vol. 11, No. 2, Winter 1995, p. 2.
3. R.S. Pathak, "Feminist Concerns in Shobha De's *Snapshots*", *Points of View*, *op. cit.*, p. 90.
4. Rosalind Coward, "This Novel Changes Women's Lives: Are Women's Novels Feminist Novels", in *Feminist Review*, 5 (1980), p. 230.
5. Toril Moi, "Feminist Literary Criticism", *Modern Literary Theory*, eds. Ann Jafferson and David Robey (London: B.T. Batsford Ltd., 1986), p. 208.
6. Simon de Beauvoir, *The Second Sex* (1949), Trans. H.M. Parshley (Penguin, 1983), p. 445.

7. T.N. Singh, "Feminism and Fiction", *Feminism and Recent Fiction in English*, ed. Sushila Singh (New Delhi: Prestige Books, 1991), p. 11.
8. Alfred Tennyson, *The Princess* (1847), *The Works of Alfred Lord Tennyson*, II (London: Macmillan & Co., 1984), p. 78.
9. Kamala Das, *Summer in Calcutta* (New Delhi: Everest Press, 1965), p. 52.
10. Quoted in Jaya Banerjee's Review of The Vintage Book of Feminism: *The Essential Writings of the Contemporary Women's Movement*, ed. Miriam Schneir Vintage (Distri. Rupa & Co.), *The Hindu*, 2 July 1995, p. XIII.
11. Julia Kristeva, "Women's Times", quoted in *Points of View, op. cit.*, p. 5.
12. Chaman Nahal, "Feminism in English Fiction: Forms and Variations", *Feminism and Recent Fiction in English*, ed. Sushila Singh, *op. cit.*, p. 17.
13. *Ibid.*, p. 15.
14. *Ibid.*, p. 19.
15. *Ibid.*
16. *cf.*, J.P. Tripathi has truthfully written in this connection: "Both Anita Desai and Shashi Deshpande explore human relationships in modern Indian society, particularly the husband-wife relationship. Shashi Deshpande's women, like those of her predecessor, are tolerant, obedient and submissive. But a feminist awakening and upsurge is all along notable in their feelings and conduct" in his article "The Feminist Surge in Jaya's Ego" in Shashi Deshpande's *That Long Silence*, in *Points of View*, Vol. II, No. 2, Winter 1995, p. 80.
17. R.S. Pathak, "Feminist Concerns in Shobha De's *Snapshots*", *Points of View, op. cit.*, p. 90.
18. Shobha De, "Sex in the Time of Stress" in Khushwant Singh and Shobha De (eds.) *Uncertain Liaisons: Sex, Strife and Togetherness in Urban India* (Delhi Viking/Penguin India, 1993), pp. XXI, 208.
19. Shobha De quoted in *Points of View, op. cit.*, p. 101.

3

Early Phase: The Indian Women

Ruth Prawer Jhabvala's novels to date may be convincingly divided into three phases—each bearing on the issues of romantic idealism, the shedding of illusion and the search for wholeness of womanhood. Since her fiction centers around women and she observes the issues that feminism grapples with, there is a live portrayal of the feminine sensibilities and their quest for identity in the patriarchal society that renders them effectively powerless. This chapter tends to present an analytical portrayal of the feminine sensibilities in her early novels having exclusively Indian women and conservative social system. This phase of Indian womanhood covers her first five novels—*Amrita: To Whom She Will* (1955), *The Nature of Passion* (1956), *Esmond in India* (1957), *The Householder* (1960) and *Get Ready for Battle* (1962).

With the exception of *Esmond in India* these novels are not generally involved with Europeans but portray Indian families and predicament of women with lights of modernity coming on. The first two novels *To Whom She Will* and *The Nature of Passion* treat the theme of disillusionment in its gentlest and most benign form: the comic mismatching of pairs of lovers who, as the novels progress, discover the difference between illusions and hard realities. The women protagonists are thwarted by their own romantic idealism, by the economic realities and by a social system that devalues them.

To Whom She Will was reissued in the United States as *Amrita* but the British title is explicated by an epigraph taken from a Vedic epic *Panchatantra* in translation, by H. Ryder:

For if she bids a maiden still,
She gives herself to whom she will,
Then marry her in tender age
So warns the Heaven-begotten sage.[1]

This warning of heavenly sage rests unheard in the case of Amrita who, valiantly, if naively, attempts to give herself to whom she will, thereby hangs the plot of the novel probing the tender core of feminine heart and mind. The plot of *To Whom She Will* appears to endorse the wisdom of that institution dear to original conservatism; the marriages arranged by family elders between young people who lack the experience or are denied the opportunity to choose partners for themselves. Amrita Chakravorty finds her otherwise westernized upper-class relations uncongenial, who think her in love with Hari Sahni—a poor young Punjabi working at New Delhi Radio Station where she is a part-time announcer. Amrita's grandfather, though not deadly against the marriage outside the immediate community, forbids this marriage because there is a gulf between their social status and family backgrounds. He warns Amrita as: "But in your case, the margin, the discrepancy between the two families, the young man's and yours, is too wide. It is a gulf that I cannot find it in my conscience to allow you to bridge."[2]

Her mother Radha and her aunts begin to search for a socially acceptable suitor for her. Amrita suffers the blows of social bondages and she is afflicted with an inner division on this issue of her marriage. There is no one whom Amrita could confide in and trust and she has to rely only on herself. Although Amrita seems more sensible, more tactful, less noisy and vociferous than her mother, her cautiousness and self-consciousness are attributed to her upbringing and to her schooling at Lady Wilmont College. She is timid yet demonstrates defiance, innately cautious yet prepared for recklessness, primly refined yet unhappy with refinement, English by training yet Indian by predilection. For instance, her feelings battered against the convention which forbade her to go herself to Hari's house. But she doesn't have the courage to override it, as her too much modesty, her training, her tradition, are too strong for her. Amrita's arrogance bursts in chapter eight when she speaks to Krishna. "Everybody is always telling us to be emancipated, to be like European women; but when we try to be they are shocked and say we are behaving badly" (*To Whom She Will*, p. 49).

The author's second choice of the title, i.e. *To Whom She Will* places the heroine at the centre and underlines the fact that on a more important thematic level the novel is a story about maturing and refinement of the sensibility of a young woman whose fanciful feelings for Hari are based on an idealized concept of the Indianness. Ruth Jhabvala likes to develop a plot in which the romantic love is less than adequate. Although Jhabvala extracts much comedy from the romantic excesses of these sentimental lovers and portrays the conflict between youth and age, the dominant shades of the picture she draws are that of the Indian family as a loving protective 'cocoon' above all other considerations. Yasmine Goonaratne endorses this view—

> We may detect here an indirect assertion that Amrita itself is a novel in which the style adopted and the sensibility expressed are native and natural to the author and her subject neither borrowed nor assumed.[3]

On the other hand, Hari's family also realises the ground realities and drags him back to the tradition of the arranged marriage within their status. His mother proclaims, "He is a good son, he will marry a nice girl you will see; one of our own girls whom his family will choose for him" (*To Whom She Will*, p. 13). Hari, for whom being in love, of course, was wonderful, not only wonderful but also necessary, makes inadequate resistance against the family decision to get him married with the daughter of Anand's family. He only says "I can not marry when I love another" (*To Whom She Will*, p. 95).

Hari looks miserable and perplexed: he knows he must not displease his family and he also knows that he must not betray his love for Amrita. Even that his love is at present beset with and entangled in so many difficulties; Amrita's grandfather, the mother, thoughts of police and prison: and now, worst of all the displeasure of his own family. Hari's family wastes no time in negotiating a marriage settlement for him with the Anand's family and Hari, after a little resistance, surrenders to the pressure of his own family. Hari Sahni is booked for Sushila Anand in the business-like way that a prize bull would be purchased for a stock-breeder's herd.

Even Amrita who rates her romantic love very high gradually realises the dominance of the traditional arrangements, conservatism and economic considerations in her so-called westernized family. She eventually accepts the companionship in marriage with Krishna Sen Gupta, the Bengali intellectual. It is merely an irony of situation that in the beginning Amrita neglects this Bengali boy who has already declared his love for her but eventually she begins to love him by the time her mother plans an arranged marriage between these two young persons whom only similarity that binds is community.[4] Worn out, by family pressure Hari sacrifices Amrita's love and even Amrita gradually becomes aware of the practical feasibility of the partner from a socially suitable background. Thus, as per title the novel emphasizes the family match making and stratagem as the dominant plot. We also agree that inner strains and stresses, romantic instincts and heartfelt emotions of woman are futile cries in this over-possessive society of India.[5]

The views expressed by these relatives suffer from self-deception of various kinds and personal concerns not connected with Amrita's or Hari's happiness. The question whether arranged or love marriages are most conducive to happiness remains unresolved even at the end of the novel. Sunk is a lassitude from which nothing can awaken them, the older generation cannot appreciate their youngsters' need to think and act as individuals with their own sense and sensibility. Within this ambiguous but generally compassionate picture of youth and age in conflict, Jhabvala finds the traumatic picture of feminine sensibility being crushed and humiliated mainly by womenfolk themselves. The supreme irony on the question of marriage is probably at the moment when after many hours of negotiation in which no thought of love or mutual affection has entered, Hari is booked for Sushila Anand. Jhabvala intends to expose the utter insensitivity of elders to the delicate feelings of their young children. Ironically, the young persons are passive in these arrangements. While Hari has no honesty or the strength of will to oppose what is being done to him Amrita is more straightforward and declares her plan to go to England to avoid an early marriage.

Three principal characters of this novel, Amrita, Hari and Krishna Sen Gupta, present a series of interesting contrasts. All of them on the threshold of maturity simultaneously reflect their individual sensibility and influence of their social milieu on their personality. Hari, sociable, warmly appreciative of a pretty face and figure is described by an amused patronizing friend as a true son of India. Caught between Amrita's love and his filial ties, he wishes to please everyone and to offend nobody but ultimately submits himself to the wish of his parents. The maturity to which the novel's events bring him is neither intellectual nor moral but physical only. At the height of betrothal celebration Hari thinks of his vows of fidelity to Amrita but, strangely enough, he also feels his own growing bodily desire for Sushila Anand. Jhabvala lashes the hypocritical masquerading of Hari as a noble self-sacrificing being which in reality is self-deception of him.

Amrita's other admirer Krishna Sen Gupta is repelled at the start of his acquaintance with her by her complete mental innocence what he called her prudery, her shy disregard for his own sex. Her failure to see in him anything but a brotherly presence in her mother's house rankles though he pretends not to care. Krishna, though partially a product of his upbringing, has inherited the idealism and intellectualism which leads him towards an independent point of view. On Hari's assertion that he will not be alive without Amrita, Krishna's unspoken assessment of this Romeo comes amusingly close to the truth of his false avowals. Amrita, still in love with Hari, realises the inefficiency of Hari's emotions and becomes aware of Krishna's importance in her life. The gradual shift of Amrita's affection from Hari to Krishna is delicately and comically portrayed.

In Amrita some traits are imbibed from her traditional background but others are more personal and individual which make this character shine far above her lover who is not sincere to his deep emotional need of love. Amrita's quietness before her relations' opposition to her love is far more eloquent as it hides a resolution and strength of will that emerges in her firm resistance to her mother's duplicity and the tyranny of her grandmother's duplicity and turbulent feelings. In reality, she is not prepared to submit yet and her courage and resolution are far greater than that of her lover and it is because of him that she has also no option but to return with relief into her promising relationships in her own community.

It is one of Jhabvala's triumphs in this early novel that refined sensibility and moral truths of a woman protagonist in conflict with other women of traditional society are clinically dissected in scene after scene without distorting social verisimilitude or disturbing the comic equilibrium of the work as a whole. The final chapter of this novel links all the characters together in final accord and happiness all around. It is Ruth Jhabvala's first novel and never again will she write so light hearted a story. The attractive and high principled heroine ultimately finds a husband who understands her best and loves her most deeply; the rejecting and rejected Hari finds joy in his arranged marriage. Pandit Saxena renews his beliefs in his own importance and Radha looks forward with pleasure to bringing about the match that has just arranged itself through mutual esteem. No violence is intended and no real violence is offered.

The second novel *The Nature of Passion* also handles the genuine social problems of women in the Indian joint families. Corruption in business and in the Indian bureaucracy and materialistic approach to the feelings and emotions of womenfolk alongwith their vanity is articulated from a woman's point of view. The novel presents a fictional world that is though rich in humour, colour and interest yet a symbol of male rapacity on a vast scale. Its title implies an attempt on Ruth Jhabvala's part to penetrate the passions of the Indian women and to express them in her own feminine terms. From the first paragraph of the novel the tension between tradition and modernity is established and Jhabvala picturises the morally, intellectually and aesthetically bleak characters dominating the scene. *The Nature of Passion* is a sarcastic exposure of the worldliness on one hand and the attitude of a rapacious man towards women on the other.[6]

Lalaji is obviously a rich and an old-fashioned man trying to keep pace with the changing world. His ruling passion emerges as an eagerness to extend his influence and power through a growing network of family and business connections. He has an unfailing interest in the worldly advancement of his children whom he considers as extension of himself. The novelist creates the crooked world of this businessman who enlists our unwilling admiration for the determination with which he rules his wayward family remaining true to his own practical view of life. But it is ironical that for him modernity is limited to his selfish standards of law and morality whereas his attitude towards women is conservative and degrading one. His attitude towards his wife is not of any emotional type but he needs her there to perform her wifely duties. In other words, his wife is treated by Lalaji as merely another possession that he has acquired. He believes that whether a household is rich or poor, the life of women is always the same. The women have a life apart in the courtyard and see to the cooking and children. When Lala Narayan Das muses about the marriage of his most beloved daughter Nimmi, Jhabvala forcefully underlines the subservient position of woman in Indian social setup as:

> A woman is a woman and her duties in life are very different from the duties of a man...it is a woman's fate to leave the house of her father and go to a husband's house, to bear his children, to look to the comforts of his family.[7]

The admirable objectivity with which Jhabvala dissects the sensibilities of women characters makes it possible for us to see *The Nature of Passion* as a satiric exposure to the worldliness on the one hand and probe into female psyche on the other.

The birth of a daughter to Lalaji's eldest son Om brings the family and its clan connections together in a spirited display of community loyalty and jubilation and introduces the principal characters of the novel. Ved, the younger son and the youngest daughter Nimmi show, by their behaviour on such an occasion that they are in revolt against the family traditions which, they feel, are a threat to their individuality. The reader is unobtrusively shown the source from which conflict can be anticipated to arise: the children's desire for independence will clash in turn with their father's wish to direct their future along the path chosen by himself and thus contributing to the number and prosperity of the clan.

Lalaji believes that he has erred in educating his son Chandra abroad. As a result, he has acquired, in place of a respectful and biddable extension to his family, a modern daughter-in-law who despises his overpossessive parentage. In Lalaji's world woman has a subservient status inside the four walls of the household. We see an ironic and satirical treatment of Indian women as expressed in this novel:

> A family was not a family, a home not a home, unless there was a women's quarter in which the women could lead their own lives. Demure daughters-in-law, stern mothers-in-law, widowed aunts, all pounding spices, sifting rice, scolding servants, washing babies,...these constituted the necessary, if unconsidered, background to a man's life. (*The Nature of Passion*, p. 112)

When Jhabvala describes the birth of Om's third child—a girl-baby, another item has been added in Lalaji's long list of expensive possessions. Om, though belonging to a generation ahead of his father, is not different in defining an exactly similar role for his daughter. Pointing to his six-year old child, he says:

> When she is seven, I will find a good husband and betroth her. Then she can come back to the house and learn from her mother and aunts to make chapatis and mango pickle. When she has learnt that well, and also how to manage servants and children, she can go to her

husband's house and be credit to us there. (*The Nature of Passion*, p. 16)

These plans for a child who has not even got the first glimpse of the world are humorous yet appalling. Can there be questions of identity and equality of the sexes in such stifling and socially predetermined world? These traditional codes of womanhood are challenged by the straightforward rebellionness of Nimmi who trembles with fury at this affront of woman education. Nimmi, almost a reincarnation of Amrita of *To Whom She Will*, is Lalaji's favourite daughter and stands apart from the crowd as she yearns to be elegant and cultured. She goes to college; has a number of friends from the upper circles of society; is exposed to the club culture and at the same time is aware of the difference between their sophisticated world and hers—a difference which she realises money alone can not bridge. She is quite critical and disapproving of all the women in her household except Kanta, her sister-in-law whom she tries to emulate. Kanta, the wife of Chandra Prakash, is a girl from a different community and gives enough cause to the women of the household to raise their eyebrows at her disapprovingly. Yet this modern idea of a nuclear family—Chandra Prakash lives in a separate house breaking the joint family system—is, therefore, only half-formed but Nimmi is able to get in Kanta's household all that she finds lacking in her father's house. Kanta maintains and carries herself well, speaks good English, sends her children to an English school, throws parties at her house, holds membership of a club and even smokes and drinks at times. She is thus poles apart from Shanta the other daughter-in-law of Lalaji who is docile and subservient.

Nimmi is a woman with a difference from the other womenfolk in Lalaji's family. She has no desire to become (as her mother and sister-in-law Shanta have) the part of the unconsidered background and appendage to the life of a man. She also disdains the status of women in her family and has no respect but contempt for her sister-in-law whose whole existence is concentrated on Om but she herself is ignored and belittled by him. Nimmi revolts and rebels against the confines of this tradition bound society. She cuts her hair causing an uproar in the family. The foremost worry in the women's quarter is how a husband would be found for her now. Her mother and Phuphiji, the most rigid and conservative women of the house, are much offended. They all blame Lalaji for having been too indulgent and lenient with her. But there is no stopping to the bold strides of this girl. She goes to the club with her friends and plays tennis dressed in shorts, drinks sherry even though it tastes like petrol, has a Parsi boyfriend and even allows him to kiss her in the moonlight. In addition to all these rebellious acts of hers Jhabvala notices some other effects that this desire for emancipation has caused on her mind.

Nimmi's defiant attitude and unconventional behaviour is labelled as disrespect and immodesty and has raised the whole women quarter up in arms against her. Their patience boils over when Shanta's mother reports that Nimmi had been seen going around with a Parsi boy in a night club. Lalaji is at once summoned from the office alongwith Om. A reader can almost recall an identical incident in *To Whom She Will*, when Amrita's father is made to intervene by Radha to stop her affair with Hari. Disgrace has fallen on Lalaji's family because Nimmi has been allowed to become eighteen years old and no husband found for her. Phuphiji cries vengefully, 'A girl of that age has no right to enjoy herself! She should be managing a household and bringing children and looking after a husband'; Lalaji responds with mild pity, 'It will come to her soon enough' (*The Nature of Passion*, p. 164). A verdict is passed—'take the girl away from the college.... She must stay at home here with us and not move out of the women's quarters' (*ibid.*).

Jhabvala describes Lalaji as a man accustomed to old ways yet trying to make way for the new. Even now he has no doubt but there is other danger of the news spreading and her name being maligned. So the only thing to do when there is a threat to the reputation is to find a husband, quickly, at once, before the canker spreads. A husband is found, a marriage is fixed and it is remarkable that Nimmi agrees to it after a few initial fanciful bursts of ideas like running away and becoming a teacher. It is a bit difficult to believe this change in a girl who had defiantly stated that if her marriage were arranged like that of Usha's she would spurn it aside. Describing how she would do this, she had said:

> I will never say 'yes' if they come to me with a husband they have kindly found for me. On the contrary I will tell them: Thank you, I am grateful to you for your trouble, but if you do not mind I will find my own husband. This is a work I will do for myself. (*ibid.*, p. 154)

Quite ironically the reverse of what she stated, actually happens. There are two reasons for Nimmi's submission to her family's wish. The first is her disappointment with her lover Pheroze who sends his congratulations on her engagement. She is unable to comprehend this behaviour of her sweetheart lover that he should be willing to lose her altogether. On this Nimmi takes a practical view of this frivolous romance. Moreover, it is worth observing in Nimmi that her claims for superiority and her own standards are superficial; she plans merely to be more fashionable and to marry someone better-looking. Her feelings for Pheroze Batliwala, her first love, are based on curiousity rather than on any mutual bondage. She wishes to be admired and envied and picks up Pheroze as a boyfriend and even when he kisses her in the moonlight at Qutub Minar she does not think of love: rather her mind is busy recording the experience: "So this is how a man kisses—and next: what would they say at home?—and next: How excited Rajen will be when she hears" (*ibid.*, p. 104).

Despite her wish, as a student of Keats, to appreciate the difference between 'sensuality' and 'sensuousness' Nimmi really does not understand what is meant by love or genuine intimacy. In this no-win situation, Nimmi's wishes are not regarded by women of the house and she, in spite of all her flighty behaviour, bows to the family. Kanta does nothing to help the girl in her predicament except labeling her as another victim of society. Rani, with her face flushed, declares she would not return to her husband's house until something is done about Nimmi and the disgrace she has brought to her family. In the long line of Jhabvala's pseudo-modern women, it is only Rajen, Nimmi's friend, who lends voice to some of the most feminist utterances in the novel. Throughout the novel, quite indirectly Jhabvala has been giving us glimpses of a parallel process which is taking shape in which women like Nimmi and Rajen are clamouring, though in vain, as individuals in their own rights. Once Nimmi's marriage is fixed, she draws consolation from this substitute in Kuku since for Nimmi, too, marriage has become the ultimate goal in life. Jhabvala however in Nimmi gives us a glimpse of the stirrings within the Indian womenfolk, of desires which leap beyond the confining walls of the home, of longings for a share in the world beyond and of a quest for an identity of their own. Though in the end the male factor threatens to swamp Nimmi's identity, yet she succeeds in making an indelible impression on the reader's mind. We remember her as a fresh breath of spring—as Nimmi—not as Lalaji's daughter or Kuku's wife. The novel offers an implicit criticism of the position of women in the Indian joint family; corruption in Indian bureaucracy and business and so many other defects of the system in India.[8]

Ruth Jhabvala's fiction characteristically focuses on India in which she finds herself at that time of and *Esmond in India* is no exception. Published in 1957 it again depicts the urban upper middle-class India in which, ten years after independence, life has adjusted to the realities of Swaraj. The former revolutionaries like Har Dayal are somewhat out of date and their places are being taken by the younger generation which is full with a passion for freedom but still in bondage of social tradition. The fact that *Esmond in India* ends as it begins, by focusing on Shakuntala's girlish enthusiasm for life and later on for love, demonstrates that Jhabvala's novels are not historical, rather their action took place in the shadow or the aftermath of the great event of independence. The chief interest of the novel lies in the inward perceptions of the characters; in their capacity of self-knowledge and self-deception, and their impulse towards self-fulfilment or self-destruction.

The protagonist here is again a woman—Shakuntala—but as usual she is in the protective and possessive cocoon of her parents. The principal characters comprise Esmond Stillwood a foreigner (for the first time in Jhabvala's novels) and different members from four households of Indian society. The plot brings these households of Har Dayal, Ram Nath, Uma and Esmond—into alternate association and conflict as Gulab becomes engaged to Har Dayal's son Amrit, and then marries Esmond, returning at the end of the novel with her son Ravi to her mother Uma's house; as Shakuntala is thought of as a suitable wife for Narayan by his mother Uma, but she has a love affair with Esmond.

Esmond is the only European among the Indians from four households. He is only linked with Uma's family by a formal bond of marriage with her daughter Gulab though they all disapprove this marriage which Gulab entered in with her initial attraction for this westerner. In spite of the fact that Gulab's marriage was already fixed with Amrit and her mother Uma was deadly against this affiliation of her daughter with this culturally inappropriate westerner, Gulab herself decided to marry him after attending some lectures delivered by him in college. Uma is much disturbed on this step of her only daughter and her arrogance bursts out before her brother Ram Nath when he enquires about Gulab's life. Uma speaks with arrogance and hopelessness. "What was there to tell?" she said, "I could speak only to God in my prayers, no one else knows what moves a mother's soul."[9]

Gulab, who in her initial attraction for Esmond and her later opposition to him becomes a symbol of India as far as he is concerned, adopts a way of life that is in appropriate conflict and contrast with Esmond's western sense and sensibility. The plot portrays mutual attraction turning into mutual repulsion leading to disillusionment and alienation. Esmond seems to be manifested with a colonial superiority of whiteman being benevolent in attempting to improve his Indian wife Gulab. Five years ago, when they were first married, Esmond had taken her everywhere. She hated going out since it was not a part of her upbringing and so unacceptable to her sedate though serene sensibility. From this juncture the bickering in their family life started. Jhabvala explains quite sympathetically that "he found that her absence was far more impressive than her presence" (*Esmond in India*, p. 34).

Gradually his growing distaste for India merges with contempt for his lovely and slow-witted wife until she becomes, in his overwrought imagination, the living embodiment of all he resents and despises about India. Gulab's sleepiness seems to oppose his alert rationality; her lethargy to his energetic activity, her quiet complacence to his need for lively companionship. Gulab is also an embodiment of Indian loyalty of a woman to her husband and cannot even think of any other man except him. But contrary to her Esmond pays least respect to this aspect of her personality and wishes her to be exciting and charming at any cost. Esmond finds occasional relief from his family problems by flirting with other women.

Shakuntala, the fashionable, romantic and modern girl, seems an oasis to Esmond in his dry life in India. She happened to meet him in a cocktail party. Ruth Jhabvala defines Shakuntala's craze for experiencing the life of freedom and romance. Shakuntala has been much interested in Esmond, ever since Gulab married him and she was fanciful what he could be like, this unknown Englishman who has taken Gulab away from Amrit. Her curiosity is satisfied now and in freedom of the enjoyment she holds out her hand which Esmond has to shake. Their affair develops and only a few days later she wishes to relish the company of Esmond in loneliness and a freedom of enjoyment. When Esmond struggles to liberate himself from India his personality begins to disintegrate along with the bickerings in his marriage as the strain of living with Gulab becomes more and more intense. Jhabvala describes their predicament of disharmony and hatred: "He was trapped, quite trapped. Here in this flat which he had tried to make so elegant and charming, but which she had managed to fill completely with her animal presence. His senses revolted at the thought of her..." (*Esmond in India*, p. 207).

Infatuated with Esmond and never guessing that his picturesque melancholy goes far deeper than mere disappointment in a dull wife, Shakuntala thinks divorce of Esmond and Gulab the perfect answer to her hope to marry her English lover. Fearlessly holding his hand in a crowded shopping street, Shakuntala still undeceived by reality, tells herself she knows life to be wonderful, a hundred times even more wonderful than she had expected. To the reader who has been admitted by the novelist to the secret plan of Shakuntala's parents to arrange her marriage and the desire of Esmond to evade India, it is of course clear that reality of life will not lead itself to her romantic extravagance. The six months of her glorious freedom she enjoyed since her graduation, are about to end in a traditional turn as she is to enter in a socially approved marriage bond with the Harvard—returned son of her father's friend. Shakuntala's affair creates nothing but comic pleasure to the reader because even in her freedom to aspire for Esmond, she is utterly slavish with a desire to be enthralled by this man of her choice:

> Esmond, I know you are married and also you have a child, but I tell you all this means nothing to me. Only I know you have come into my life and now it is my duty to give everything I have to you, to adore you and to serve you and to be your slave. (*Esmond in India*, p. 148)

But all her romantic dreams are destined to be shattered because the traditions are still dominant in this so-called modern household of her father. Shakuntala, who had pitied at her sister-in-law at the start of the novel, soon finds all choices and possibilities, including her dream of daring marriage with Esmond closed forever. Unlike Jane Austen's heroine Emma Woodhouse, Shakuntala does not grow up into good sense and sensibility. At the end of the novel she is very much what she was at its beginning, spoiled, self-centred and a little obtuse. All that her romantic wonderful experience of life has given her is a romantic memory of her love affair with Esmond to carry into the safe, conventional life she will lead as young Mrs. Bhatnagar in Delhi socialite.

Like Jhabvala's previous two novels, this also depicts a mental and psychological bondage of Indian women that is far more difficult for them to break in spite of all desires for freedom and excitements for self-realisation. Gulab and Shakuntala have left mere conventions behind them in their expression of love yet, they appear to be more effectively bound by their upbringing, social restraints and innate Indian sensibility than by any formal rule of purdah. Ram Nath, despite his irritation with Laxmi, understands the inescapable dilemma of the Indian women at large.

Though these women have not been radical enough, yet they have succeeded in creating ripples in the serene, sedate, and predetermined lives of the tradition-bound women of India. These shallow, pretentious, pseudo-intellectual westernized young socialites, increasingly becoming a part of modern India, expose the narrow, restricted and insufficient sense in which women's emancipation and modernity is being interpreted by Indian people. Moreover, selfish preoccupations of different kinds lurk behind Shakuntala's demonstrative affection for her father; Gulab's dependence on Uma; Madhuri's approval of Amrit and Lakshmi's defensive advocacy of Narayan. Only Uma is set a little apart from other women by her idealism and the genuine warmth of her nature for national freedom. Yet once the unusual stimulus of the freedom struggle is withdrawn, even this vigorous female personality reverts to the type-wasting her uncommon energies in hostility towards her foreign son-in-law and in overprotective care of her daughter and grandson. These women who consider themselves free are, in reality, quite slaves to traditions and worldly matters. The single character in the novel, who appears to have found true freedom of spirit, is Ram Nath's brilliant son Narayan, who is a physician and has given up wealth, comforts and social appraisal in order to work among the poor in the countryside. But this ideal young man gets no suitable match to be married, no affection and pride of mother, he gets only the indifferent treatment from all the women in his family circle. So the free India in which these women move in conflict and occasional association is itself ideologically unsettled and confused. The old struggle of Indian nationalism versus British imperialism has given place to a new conflict between tradition and modernity and woman is still without any identity as an individual.

Old values seem to be evaporating but no new social ideology has yet shaped in India of post-independence. In the world of shifting values, Ruth Jhabvala sets herself to depict certain women characters at different stages and degrees of their sensibilities. Indian classical music and literature, devotional songs, dance, and art stand in these early novels for the essential and most valuable aspect of Indian culture and her characters especially women, reveal their inner aesthetic sense to the readers according to their capacity to respond to these aspects of India.

In *The Householder*, Ruth Prawer Jhabvala tells a story about one of the four *Ashramas* of human life which is the most crucial of the four prescribed in classics of Indian culture. The household is the second stage in the life of man or woman following the first of the child studenthood and preceding the last two stages associated with withdrawal from active life and shifting towards contemplation. The focus in this novel is narrowed as it deals with the struggle of a young pair to establish their household and earn a good living to strengthen their social status and internal integration of family life.

The novel begins with Prem in a newly occupied flat and he is with his newly-wed wife Indu. This is the kind of personal exile which generally occurs in Indian society when a young man is married and he has to set up a new independent household for his wife. This is the ordeal of his *purushartha*—manliness—in the eyes of his wife as well as the society at large. At this juncture of life Prem finds himself lacking the financial resources to prove his self-sufficiency and identity as an honourable householder. Prem is not a giant but a child by experience and wisdom of life and Indu discerns this lacking of *purushartha* in the personality of her husband. He is burdened with a teaching job and in his dealing with the college principal, the colleagues, the students and the people outside, he is always aware of his inferior position which he finds irrecoverable. But inside his house he deliberately resorts to his father's brand of stern authoritarianism in order to disguise his own weakness and vulnerability. Indu understands this behavioral manifestation of her husband who has no means of protecting himself in difficult encounters of life.

Lacking the wiles and guiles or the resourcefulness needed for subterfuge, Prem is almost the perfect victim, a plaything, for the people and an inadequate husband for Indu. He suffers from a complex of unsuitability and inability in facing the new challenges of his life; such as his having to face his employer the principal Mr. Khanna to ask for a raise in salary or his having to face his landlord Mr. Seigal to request a reduction in his rent. Indu's enthusiasm for a new married life has evaporated and she feels fatigue and tried due to the haplessness and hopelessness of her household life. Though Prem, in his heart of heart, realises that Indu is miserable only due to his inability to provide her those resources which make a woman's sense of self-blossoming. Moreover, already insufficient as a householder, he feels embarrassed when Indu gets pregnant. Prem suffers from a terrible sense of insecurity and insufficiency as he lacks self-confidence, self-defence, self-assertion and all heroic traits for which a wife worships or at least honours her husband in traditional set up of Indian society. But he is unable to collect courage for any action and faces great embarrassment on every occasion. Jhabvala remarks, "Prem is always haunted with a feeling of failure. He felt himself to be terribly inadequate as a husband, a teacher and as an adult altogether."[10]

The over-possessive and stern mother-in-law of Indu adds to the bickering in their household. The middle-aged widow directs her insolent affection towards her only son and her dominating presence and solicitude make it impossible for Prem and his wife to have private conversation and harmonious decisions of household. Indu, who is already aggrieved on the inadequacy of her childish husband, finds herself trapped and harassed even at emotional level due to this intrusion. On finding Prem still behaving like a little child of his obsessive mother Indu becomes offensive against the presence of her mother-in-law.

After a feud with Prem's mother, Indu leaves for her parents' house and Prem feels himself an utter failure. Jhabvala says:

> In his present mood it gave him a grim satisfaction to count up his various failures; he could not earn sufficient money; his career as a teacher was turning out to be unpromising; he had no real friends—even Ray who had once been a real friend, had deserted him; he was not a successful husband.... It was because he was not a successful husband and she had gone away; and he had not been able to make her obedient and respectful; if she had been obedient and respectful she would not have dared to go away. Or if she had liked him better, she would not have wanted to go away. (*The Householder*, p. 85)

With his occasional forays away from his wife Prem relapses into the stage of his bachelor-like days. At one time he aspires to live like a hermit and visits a swami for religious consolation for his failures. But the world forces him back on himself to discover within himself a public identity which may befit his new public and social role. This is the process of diversion and compartmentalization which characterises the adult world at large. Through these deviations of Indu and Prem from their household, Ruth Jhabvala appears to hint at the new dimensions of theme, which are taken up in her subsequent novels: the search for some alternative society, or human community or religious dominion, some relieving alternative to ordinary middle-class standards, values and anxieties.

When Indu returns from her parents' house she appears remote and cold finding that in her absence her mother-in-law has usurped her position as 'the lady of the house'. She, however, does not show her feelings and remains quite submissive and does not make any demand—physical or emotional on her husband. But in her heart she is determined to take her full hold and her feelings get too strong to respect the traditional rules and regulations. Even Prem appears to be coming out of the shadow of mother fixation and realises the damaging effect of his obedience to mother. He also realises that he wants to be looked after not by mother now but by a beloved wife full of mutual love. Their emotional and sexual necessity forces them at last into an oblique confession of mutual need and love.

The novelist highlights the loving moments of the mutual surrender and bliss on their reunion:

> In the night they went to sleep out on the roof. They felt both alone and supreme. Prem, forgetting all his failures and anxieties, persuades Indu to take off all her clothes and show herself naked to him. She blushed, giggled, clutched the sari defensively to her breast while he tried to pull it off. They struggled together and then they loved together, never had they known such an excess of sweetness. (*The Householder*, p. 118)

Their growing sympathy and glowing affection for each other help them to sustain their sexual relationship which is the first cementing force of a household. Now Prem and Indu begin to present to the outside world a united front that accords with accepted tradition of a household. Prem's new found maturity emerges and he decisively arranges for his mother's tactful removal from his home to that of his sister. This comes as a great relief to Indu who is eager to repossess her whole share in her husband though inadequate in his role. Jhabvala seems to convey the truth when Prem ultimately realises that it is better to be a good householder—though it is not easy—than a rotten student or a hopelessly inapt holy man. He discovers the true value of his young wife and thus of marriage and suppresses his own snobbery when faced with other girls' lack of education and culture.

The novel moves towards a resolution that woman is the pivotal figure in a household provided man proves his manliness in managing resources, fulfilling sexual needs and catering to emotional desires without any intrusion or authoritarian hold on her. Prem comes to realise this truth though only partially. Some other problems of household simply cannot be solved and are better not thought about so deeply. Prem and Indu feel the need of mutual belonging for an integrated existence. However, on the surface *The Householder* conforms to a comic pattern since it is a story dealing with youthful vitality, idealism, fancies and frustrations of an Indian middle-class couple. When the humour is overdone by the ironic vision of Ruth Jhabvala, the middle-class world appears in all too sober, even tragic in hues as the world is as it is—hard and intransigent and yielding few answers.

In *Get Ready for Battle* we find a sufficiently changed atmosphere with a new and radically different set of relationships amidst the characters. Perhaps, the title symbolizes the readiness of women for a battle for their final emancipation from the patriarchal dominance. Though the setting chosen here is again a familiar one as in *The Nature of Passion*, yet many progressive steps have been taken by this society. Unlike the previous novels we do not have a women's quarter here nor do we have subservient wives who are content to shift rice, pound spices and rear babies. Instead, the three women that we meet in *Get Ready for Battle*, namely Sarla Devi, Kusum Mehra and Mala are far from being subservient to their male counterparts. In fact, divorce, separation and woman's self-reliance are in the air. If a husband's ways of life do not suit his wife, it is no more necessary for her to stay with him; if a widow, even though a grandmother, happens to like a man, there is nothing to stop her from marrying him; if a husband neglects his wife and expects her to sit passively at home, it is too much to ask and revolt is not far behind. This is the scenario of feminine sensibilities with bold self decisions that Jhabvala unfolds and we observe an exercise of the female personalities as individuals.

Gulzarilal's middle-aged and kittenish mistress Kusum strives to bring him to the point of divorcing his estranged wife Sarla Devi and then marrying herself. Sarla Devi, as a woman of conscience and self-identity, is an excellent foil for other women, none of whom pursues any ideal higher than the advancement of their own prosperity, or happiness of their family life. Gulzarilal, though a rich and successful businessman like Lalaji of *The Nature of Passion*, is several steps ahead of him in attitude and outlook. The business party at Gulzarilal's residence; the mistress Kusum who has usurped the place of his lawful wife give an idea of the process of progressive transition going on in the Indian society. Ruth Jhabvala seems to be in a hurry to underline the fact that these are modern times now as we are made conscious of the difference at every step.

This process of modernity and life outside the four walls of household is obviously painstaking one for women who have been habitual to a passive and purdah life till now. In these overwhelming social circumstances the women have never felt easy enough but Ruth Jhabvala seems to expose them now so that they may be ready to fight their battle for achieving self-realisation and self-identity in India of modern times.

It is the symptomatic change in Indian social values that a mistress like Kusum Mehra is quite an accepted fact in the honoured household of Gulzarilal. Lest we should be misled into thinking that she is Gulzarilal's wife, Jhabvala quickly states the status of this lady in his household at the outset of the novel. It is worth amazing that this traditional society has undergone so much change that this widow, a mother, even a grandmother—is here quite comfortable in the house of a man with whom her relationship has no legal, social or moral sanction. Kusum has been maintaining this position for the past eight years but now she wants to remarry Gulzarilal because she realises that mistresses are not socially as feasible as the remarried widows are. She shuns the idea of leading a life of self-imposed penance and becoming old, wrinkled and haggard like Phuphiji in *The Nature of Passion*.

Kusum has taken a stronghold on the heart as well as the household of Gulzarilal. Now she is the strongest advocate of divorce as she tells Vishnu and Mala—Gulzarilal's son and daughter-in-law: "Dear Children, we are all modern now, we have a Hindu Code Bill, we have divorce" (*Get Ready for Battle*, p. 11). On the other hand, Gulzarilal himself is opposed to the idea of a divorce which militates against his favourite dream of himself as a successful family man and which distracts his attention from his main interest in life.

In striking contrast to these anxious seekers of self-interest, Jhabvala has projected a woman of strongly refined and benevolent sensibility in Sarla Devi—the estranged wife of Gulzarilal. She has abandoned her family and household for the sake of the destitute and downtrodden. In opposition to the luxurious world of her wealthy husband, Sarla Devi has raised her battle for the welfare of the oppressed poor people of slum areas. She shuns to be a traditionally-bound wife such as Gulzarilal wanted and expected her to be and her intensely revolutionary and otherworldly nature comes in direct conflict with her husband's materialistic and socially graded notion of life. Consequently they decide to part and Sarla Devi, with her visionary outlook becomes a strong representative of those rare women who represent the revolutionary fervour in modern India.[11]

But Jhabvala has developed this female character not fully as she remains a paper revolutionary; too saintly a figure to make any positive impact. She fights a losing battle for the dwellers of Bundi Basti who are being threatened with eviction under the pretext of slum clearance and provision of better environment. It is ironical that it is her estranged husband who is hoping to thwart her attempt by acquiring the land. Perhaps, woman is still not ready enough to fight her battle successfully in this society of male dominance. Sarla Devi seems to be losing her battle and even her request for help falls on deaf ears of her own son Vishnu. Austere and high-principled, she stands alone being intensely alive and in this ability to live every moment she falls in contrast with the lethargic Vishnu and Mala and most of the other characters in the novel. In the words of Yasmine Goonaratne:

> She is the symbol and epitome of what Ruth Jhabvala regards as the opposite reaction to the Indian greed and callousness she describes in her article—The Indian Spirituality—not grabbing at the world but wanting nothing whatsoever to do with it.[12]

As a woman of conscience Sarla Devi is an excellent foil for the other women characters in the novel as none of them pursues any higher ideal in life except finding their fulfillment in marriage, home and children. Sarla Devi's quest for spiritual freedom and devotion to the cause of the poor is thought of as an abnormal behaviour by her own relations. Two of them who call her 'a mad woman' are her brother Brijmohan and her daughter-in-law Mala, who is diametrically opposed to Sarla Devi. Mala's possessiveness of her husband Vishnu stands in sharp contrast with Sarla Devi's detached and indifferent attitude towards her husband Gulzarilal. Mala can be seen as a prototype of traditional Indian housewives. This was the consideration which Gulzarilal took at the time of selecting her for his son. But Mala is so much possessive that when Vishnu stays away from home to avoid his father's business work, she resents it as she frets and fumes at being neglected and turns into a virtual tigress with biting teeth and clawing nails. She complains angrily "You have the office, you have your friends, you drive off in your car and do what you like, while I sit here only and wait for the day to be finished" (*Get Ready for Battle*, p. 28). These three women are the three interpretations of the progressive sensibilities of modern Indian women at different degrees of their self-actualisation.

Two minor women characters—Toto and Ushi—represent the new rising fashionable, smart and club-attending wives of modern social circles of India. These two married women are the leaders of the young generation of sociable, up-to-date and smart women of status. They move freely among the boys and even enjoy smoking cigarette and tasting liquor as a status symbol. It is they and their likes that have prompted Jhabvala to describe the modern Indian womenfolk in obliquely satirical terms and comic tone. These shallow, pretentious, pseudo-intellectual westernized young socialites increasingly become a part of modern India and expose the narrow and restricted sense in which modernity is being interpreted by such people. All along the narrative Jhabvala also attacks the dual standard of modernity being upheld by these so-called modern women. When Mala gets furious on Sumi's calling Vishnu her friend,

Sumi gives her head a grown-up toss of coquetry "Can I help it if he is fond of me?" (*Get Ready for Battle*, p. 78). Jhabvala makes subtle hints at the mask of duality slipping away from these women who are quite far away from feminine self-reliance and independent identity. Except Sarla Devi almost all other women in the novel display a dual standard and a glaring tension between the old and the new, i.e. between tradition and modernity.

An analytical and critical survey of the plots of these novels of the purely Indian phase reveals that Jhabvala, in her chosen limited range, has successfully portrayed an astonishing picture of the average middle-class Indian women of traditional household. The novelist has created a fictional world of the domestic comforts and sensuous appeal in Indian set-up but her vision is ironic and that of a social realist. These novels centre around the theme of conservatism, feminine alienation, and agony due to suppression and exploitation in a male-dominated society of patriarchal order.

However, we witness that even in the constricted and carefully segmented world of women, faint feminine stirrings and upsurges have already started in Indian society. This rebellion against the life chalked out for the fair-sex by Indian society, is obviously becoming from strong to stronger in each successive novel. The great stride towards woman emancipation has been taken. One fact emerges in these novels having Indian women as protagonists that the dominating traits of feminine awareness are progressively developing in India womenfolk. The plots of these novels reveal that knocks of modernity and woman emancipation are being experienced in middle-class society of India. Any treachery, misery and suffering caused by the males is, though unsuccessfully, yet vehemently opposed by these protagonists of Jhabvala's fiction. The milieu is that of the moneyed and privileged class of a society in which millions are still hungry. But Jhabvala with her European background, has perceptively noticed that issues like those of identity, equality and self-actualisation—the issues that have made the feminists stand up in arms against the male-dominated world—have not yet reached the average

Indian household. To say, these Indian novels of Jhabvala are spun by an initiated outsider working within a domestic world. Lourie Sucher has admirably brought out this segmentation of theme in the early novels of Jhabvala:

> The outrage, the concern with social injustice that will appear later, is for now put aside, as if to acquaint the western audience with the urban middle class and aspects of Indian life that come less readily to mind.[13]

The protagonists of these early novels have another trait in common; they are almost completely alienated and their cry for self-realisation is not treated sympathetically by other women in their surroundings. The truth of these early cheerful novels of Jhabvala is that they are not specially cheerful at all; or rather their cheerfulness is continually undercut by a darker view of life. It is ironical that the actual stress, suppression and vulnerability to the woman is caused only by other women who are having a stronghold in households but in actuality they are indirectly executing the will and wish of the males in this patriarchal and traditional social setup. Women struggling for their identity do not, by and large, have the support, love or friendship of their own category, and therefore, are made to suffer from emotional suffocation, inconsistency, isolation and dilemma of self-pity. The traditional society of India places woman in a position of dependence and servitude to man and these novels have portrayed the feministic upsurge to come out of this bondage. The social documentation is precise and the Indian ethos is captured mainly through explication.

NOTES

1. Quoted in Lourie Sucher, "Introduction: Ruth Prawer Jhabvala and her Fiction", *The Fiction of Ruth Prawer Jhabvala: The Politics of Passion* (London: Macmillan Press Ltd., 1989), p. 14.
2. Ruth Prawer Jhabvala, *To Whom She Will* (London: Penguin Books, 1985), p. 7.
3. Yasmine Goonaratne, *Silence, Exile and Cunning: The Fiction of Ruth Prawer Jhabvala* (Hyderabad, New Delhi: Orient Longman Ltd., 1983), p. 32.
4. *cf.* Neeta Gupta endorses this point 'Modernity in its true sense of roles and rules is still a far cry. Yet what we do see in Jhabvala's novels are the first indications of a desire to overthrow the bondage to be

independent, to revolt even though it may materialise in something as inconsequential as having one's long hair cut short, *op. cit.*, p. 59.

5. *cf.* Yasmine Goonaratne's comment on the overpossessive behaviour of Indian "Ignorant and uncaring of the path Amrita's feelings have taken, her grandfather, mother and aunts will complacently view her final choice of a husband as a vindication of their own wisdom and experience", *op. cit.*, p. 34.
6. *cf.* Yasmine Goonaratne, "Ruth Jhabvala portrays the characters of this novel with a verve-recording quirks and oddities, the weaknesses and strengths of each individual in the extended (and continually extending) family of Lala Narayan Das Verma and in her anti-hero's character with its blending of endearing and repulsive qualities, we may see both a symbol of his creator's conflicting feelings for India, and evidence of her ability to externalise them in her art", *op. cit.*, p. 87.
7. Ruth Prawer Jhabvala, *The Nature of Passion* (London: Penguin Books, 1956), p. 112.
8. Yasmine Goonaratne, *op. cit.*, p. 85.
9. Ruth Prawer Jhabvala, *Esmond in India* (Middlesex, London: Penguin Books Ltd., 1980), p. 29.
10. Ruth Prawer Jhabvala, *The Householder* (London: Penguin Books Ltd., 1980), p. 53.
11. *cf.* Lourie Sucher, "In *Get Ready for Battle*, Sarla Devi (whose name derives from the Sanskrit for 'simplicity', fights stubbornly with her traditional, but proudly up-to-date family over issues of social justice, activism, and reform-concepts alien to the traditional Hindu ethos, and deriving, of course, from modern democratic idealism." *The Fiction of Ruth Prawer Jhabvala: The Politics of Passion* (London: Macmillan Press Ltd., 1989), p. 16.
12. Yasmine Goonaratne, *op. cit.*, p. 142.
13. Lourie Sucher, *op. cit.*, p. 15.

4

Middle Phase: The Western Women in Love with India and Indians

The second phase of Ruth Jhabvala's creativity covers three novels, i.e. *A Backward Place* (1965), *A New Dominion* (1972) and *Heat and Dust* (1975). Now Jhabvala's focus is on the western women and through their interaction with India and Indians the malaise of East West encounter emerges all important and most alarming in consequences. Jhabvala is now interested in delineating the predicament of the expatriate characters particularly women in the process of their living in the illusionary country India. Here it will be useful to note what Jhabvala herself has said as a confessional writer: "My work is only one individual European's attempt to compound the puzzling process of living in India."[1]

This statement made in 1972 offers useful clues to explore Jhabvala's novels of this phase and her reader whom she expects to be a westerner too, is not allowed to forget this cardinal fact. Therefore, an analytical study of the feminine sensibilities with all the manifestations and implications in this East-West interaction defines a new dimension of Jhabvala's craftsmanship as a feminine writer.

A Backward Place breaks a fresh ground of visualising India and Indians from a European feminine perspective in varying degrees and consequences. Infatuating and enchanting India is picturised and visualised in the novel through the eyes of three expatriate women. Now it is not India's problem that is central but the problems of westerners who happen to be in India after independence. Jhabvala's treatment of this socio-cultural amalgamation and confrontation from a woman's point of view is lively, sharp satirizing and ambivalent. Three expatriate women—Judy, Etta and Clarissa—represent the west in *A Backward Place* and they come in close contact with Indians. They fall in a puzzling cycle of attraction, and illusion towards everything Indian leading to disillusion and ending in frustration, self-destruction and disintegration of individual personality on the one hand or withdrawal and flight for survival on the other. David Rubin's observation is worth borrowing:

> In this case the central figures are three European women who represent in varying degrees the East-West malaise and love affairs between Indians and Europeans; the romantic vaguely questing Westerners; the adventure and flight for survival of bored, superficial and Idophobic drifters, mirrored by their egomaniacal, mindless and predatory Indian counterparts.[2]

The choice of women reflects on Jhabvala's own feminine affinity with the sensibilities and experiences of these expatriate women who have arrived in India as wives or beloveds or self-seekers on their quest for aesthetic or spiritual bliss in this country of old renown. These three women are three versions of the European sensibility at different degrees of realisation. First and foremost, there is Etta who hides her Hungarian origin by trying to put on a phoney, haw-haw English accent. She finds herself in India in consequence of her marriage to an Indian which has utterly failed. She discards Indian socio-cultural ethics which regard marriage an everlasting fusion of two souls in which woman's soul is submissive to the dominating one of man. Breaking the wedlock with her Indian husband she leads a life of permissive and sexually indulgent young woman having a long train of her lovers. For her, love is a matter of will and wish and, therefore, she has a pathetic series of transient affairs. In utter contrast to Judy who has committed to merge herself with conservative and backward social norms of her Indian husband Bal, Etta is offensive in condemning Indian norms of marriage:

> Marriages, my dear, are made to be broken, that is one of the rules of modern civilization. Just because we happen to have landed ourselves in this primitive society, that is no reason why we should submit to their primitive morality.[3]

But more than these norms Etta condemns India that has a deteriorating effect on her physical charms. As India metamorphoses all the outsiders Etta has become miserably sick to the depth of her psyche since her only asset—her looks have failed her. Etta scolds Judy for her commitment to Indian traditions and she argues that in marrying an out-of-work dreamy Indian she has committed a disastrous mistake because this will spoil and reduce her into a savage, drowned and miserable creature at last. In a loathsome and contemptuous way, she exhorts Judy:

> You are just nothing here. Look at you in that thing— Judy looked down at herself, at the sari which she mostly wore now-a-days...and your hair too and—ough you're awful. You have let yourself go. (*A Backward Place*, p. 6)

In utter despair Etta had once attempted to commit suicide on being deserted by her lovers. Finally, she takes shelter in the flat of her friend Clarissa to safeguard herself from the heat and dust of India as far as possible. She is always anxious to find a possible rescue from this country through some new lover who might be induced to finance her return to Europe. This fading Hungarian beauty, quite arrogantly, declares that life in India is nothing but awkward and intolerable:

> "There is absolutely no reason", she said, "when in Rome to do as Rome does. Or rather, there may be every reason in Rome, but certainly, certainly none in Delhi. It's no use sinking down to any one's level Judy, we must always try to raise them up to ours. Oh God, now you're making me sound like something colonial, but it's true, it really is true." (*A Backward Place*, p. 8)

Contrary to Etta is the sensibility of sincere and sober Judy who faces the challenges in the land and society of her choice. The novelist has most sympathetically drawn this character who searches the possibilities of an amicable adjustment in Indian setup. She respects her husband Bal's joint family and is patient and even foolishly happy to support her dreamy husband, his children and his aunt Bhuaji—a widow Hindu religious woman dependent on their household.[4]

In spite of all her sincerity, Judy, no doubt, feels somehow the awkwardness and futility of woman's neglected life confined to the domestic chores of the joint family. Moreover, her husband is an astrayed youngman who feeds on his hare-brain schemes and has a romantic temperament. In contrast to this indifferent and purposeless Indian, Judy is foresighted, reasonable, and keeps vigil to the needs of life. Judy's enthusiasm to absorb Indian norms of life is hurt by the rude, quarrelsome, and irritatingly false confidence of her unwise husband. Bal's violent and dominating behaviour with Judy at a public bus-stop hurts her and causes deep agony. After undergoing this traumatic experience Judy becomes scared about the atrocities and maltreatment done to women in this society of hypocritical values and ethics. She feels a jolt to her enthusiasm for Indian life and goes away from home though only for a few hours. Judy's sense of responsibility for her family, her wisdom to face the oddities of life and her stoic sensibility make her return to her husband soon after. Jhabvala highlights Judy's heroic audacity to live in poverty and adversity with patience and no idea of escapism. The narration varies from gentle irony to acid satire on this beastly and callous treatment of women in this socio-cultural drama of Indian essence. With her marriage failing and husband incorrigible, Judy is tempted to enter an adulterous relationship with an idealistic like-minded Indian colleague named Sudhir in her office. But the novelist seems to be presenting Sudhir as a temporary anchor to her feelings and emotions and she is soon saved from this sad alternative when this would-be lover of Judy leaves the corrupt Delhi to take up a teaching job in Madhya Pradesh. Then feeling ashamed by thinking about the contented resignation of her husband's pious old Bhuaji and modest dedication of her sister-in-law Shanti, Judy becomes reconciled to her otherwise silly husband.

Judy becomes a tragic figure in identifying herself with a life totally unreasonable to her refined and sedate sensibility when she stoically follows her husband to an uncertain future in Bombay. Appreciating Judy's patience and modesty C. Saros and V.A. Shahane write: "Judy perhaps is one of the few women characters in Jhabvala's fiction who strike a note of hope and affirmation in the face of unexpected and sudden change of life."[5]

Whereas Judy represents the sensible Englishness with a liberal, practical, and even phlegmatic sensibility, her another friend Clarissa is an example of an expatriate woman who fell in love with spiritual and aesthetic India—the India of Ramakrishna and Aurobindo. She is like the hippies described more acidly in *A New Dominion* and the transient European scholars who appear in minor roles in most of Jhabvala's novels often as comic or pathetic examples of India's ability to hypnotize the disillusioned westerners. She is the chief antagonist of Etta as she boasts that she has come to India out of conviction and idealism and not on a chance marriage. For her Indian life stands for the glorification of soul and she expresses her craze to experience it to Etta in these words:

> I've rejected all western values; I belong here now.... They're the most conventional, dull, bourgeois, English, English people you've ever met in your born days. God knows how I escaped being like that. We're like creatures from a different planet, absolutely. I really think I must have been Indian in my previous birth—in all my previous births.... (*A Backward Place*, p. 192)

Clarissa likes to explain her individuality as a kind of bohemianism, describing herself as an artist with an aesthetic taste. Etta and Clarissa represent two antithetical approaches of English women to India: whereas Etta needs her show of Englishness for self-protection, Clarissa feels trapped as an English woman; Etta clings to cover herself with an English mask, Clarissa tries to free herself from this same mask; Etta expresses her loathing of India, Clarissa her love of it; Etta, her skepticism, Clarissa her idealism, etc.

But nasty corruption, squalor and haplessness of the people make Clarissa's spiritual and aesthetic zeal turn into sad malaise of fragmented identity as a being. She, after experiencing the Indianness on her pulse, finds herself sick and eccentric and now desperately seeks a home in India where she could be secure from gasping landlords and the cruel impudence of street children who mock her eccentric appearance and vulnerability to insult and pillage. Yet Clarissa has acquired a certain toughness of character through her disillusionment and suffering. Though disillusioned with India, she knows that she can never return to England to confess the failure of her dreams based on India.

These three western women are engaged in a weird circling dance at the very centre of the novel, a complicated criss-crossing and an enactment which suggests some kind of private authorial rite. They present three more or less unsatisfactory solutions to the problem of being a western woman in India, which has also been the problem of Jhabvala herself. Therefore, the three women appear to be three authorial personae picturising the inner enigma of Jhabvala in pathetic manifestations. Each of these three women—wife, lesbian and kept one—face the sad discovery that India presents no solution for her. India locks all in its embrace and treats the lovers like Etta, ideal wives like Judy and aesthetic seekers like Clarissa alike as life-long prisoners here.[6]

Judy, who is the novel's hypothetical heroine, exemplifies what Ruth Jhabvala in *Myself in India* declares herself unable to do—namely to become Indian without having to surrender her own sense of Europeanness. Judy aims at merging with the Indian culture and society and, therefore, welcomes all demands that this primitive country makes upon her Europeanness. In this context Shahane's appreciation of her endeavour to harmonise the two extremes in her is quite apt and must be quoted:

> Although English by birth and alien by upbringing, she adapts herself admirably into Bal's joint family and

> the heterogenous household. She has inherited the Englishman's gift for adaptability and she adapts her western modes to the requirements and claims of Indian culture.[7]

Etta is a cynic as her personality is carefully detailed, particularly in its idiosyncrasies. The smell of India or else a stain of Indian food fills her with distaste even after a period of twenty-five years in India (exactly the period Jhabvala herself lived for in India). But Etta is a problematic personality 'a big tease' attempting to make herself cunningly seductive and good time girl who when rejected by her millionaire boy-friend Guppy (Mr. Gupta) can see no reason to come out of bed—the cage or prison.

Etta's admission "Yes, I am sick, sick, sick, sick to the depths of my soul" (*A Backward Place*, p. 214) is apparently some malady which we may not attribute to her creator who has an Indian husband and family, in spite of all her aversions to this land. In case of Clarissa, we are tempted to see the aesthetic and spiritual aspect of Jhabvala's personality finding no substantial anchoring power in this country of old renown in the field of spiritual and artistic values.

However, we are tempted to see that in this phase Ruth Jhabvala's concern to explore the expatriate individuals especially women has turned from society to the individuals of west in Indian background. The mild irony is gradually being replaced by an acid satire to attack the nasty corruption, hypocrisy and disgusting idealism or pseudo-spiritualism which dominates the next two novels of this phase.

A New Dominion renamed *Traveller* in its American edition symbolises the theme as four major western characters' journey from Delhi to the holy city of Banaras and thence to Maupur, moves deeper into India and further into experiences that put their sensibilities to severe and unexpectedly traumatic tests. *A New Dominion* is, of course, India but it is no longer the British colony that provided the setting for Forster's *A Passage to India*. Mrs. Jhabvala presents an India of new notes and rhythm reflecting sufficient change in socio-cultural perspectives.

With the dissolution of Empire the Europeans, especially women, can move freely in this new dominion which is still primitive but with no racial segregation of the rulers and the ruled. Raymond, Lee and Margaret travel with a freedom and come in close interaction with Indians unshielded by officialdom of any kind. These westerners experience joys and sorrows of unexpected intensity; heaven and hell that India's variety encompasses with her high social tradition and rich spiritual heritage.

The picturisation of contemporary India includes an incisive indictment of an Indian chauvinism that has replaced British imperial arrogance with a damaging effect upon what it contacts and controls. This assertion of *A New Dominion* takes place at many levels but most strikingly in its effect on the sensibilities of the western women who are self-seekers through Indian spiritualism at a Swamiji's Ashram. It is a sordid tale about these European women who, being tired of western materialism and boredom, come to India on a quest for self-development and spiritual rejuvenation but ironically face self-destruction and self-delusion. To their bewilderment these self-seekers are crushed and enslaved by sinister Indian forces more ruthlessly than the Indians were subjugated by the British imperialism in past. In words of Shahane who confirms author's tussle with the hard aspects of this new Indian in this novel, "*A New Dominion* tries to grapple with a vast and varied, harmonious and discordant, noble and profane reality that is India, almost inexhaustible in its range and inscrutable in its depth."[8]

India has ever been hailed as a land of spiritual heritage and this country is an abode of spiritual guides. To the westerners these spiritual values have been a great magnetic attraction which they do not find in their own land of materialistic abundance. But in modern times Indian spiritualism has gone profane at least in modern Indian godman's dominion as represented by the charismatic but sinister Swamiji. The novel projects the western view of the contemporary India as these westerners experience a whole race in its nerves, its very corpuscles that the reader may feel the truth of prevailing adverse situations. Mrs. Jhabvala, here again, takes the position of an outsider and articulates the experiences of these western women from the point of view of a woman on a quest. Her vision is ironic and even acidly sarcastic on the degradation of cultural ethics and spiritual heritage of this sub-continent.

In this novel, Ruth Prawer Jhabvala brings the Indian and the western values in colloquy through the association or conflict of the characters from distant races in the Indian setting.[9] The opening chapter of the novel i.e. *Lee Travels* symbolises the westerners' search for spiritual rejuvenation. Lee, the central figure in the trio, has a deep faith in Indian spiritual powers. Margaret, disgusted with materialism of England, its nothingness and religious aridity, has been in India for some time searching for some right guru with the hope of merging herself with glorious spiritualism. She did revolt against the commercialism, pretentiousness and falsity of the middle-class English society and refused to act her part as a bride's maid at her sister's wedding. She now turns to India and the Swamiji to quench her spiritual hunger for self-fulfillment. Now that she has found Swamiji's 'Universal Society for Spiritual Regeneration in the Modern World' she shares her excitement with Lee who follows her there to seek herself. At the Ashram Lee and Margaret share a room with Evie who is taking dictation for Swamiji's book to be called *Essence of the Upanishads.*

The new guru cult of Indian religious and spiritual guides in post-independence era is exposed with all its dubious and spell-binding hypocrisy. In this new dominion we observe the Swamiji duping innocent women and girls who have drifted away from the western materialistic world. These girls, tired of their life in hectic civilization, come to India on a quest for spiritual salvation and peace but become easy victims to the dubious guru Swamiji.

These relationships of relatively voluntary dominion and subjugation in the novel fall into two categories, though the lines between these categories blur and finally dissolve. I refer to the arenas of desire on the one hand and spiritual or religious quest on the other. The female disciples and male guru are linked in a relationship of traditionally sanctioned psychological thralldom of woman whose sexual component is only thinly veiled. Thus, these girls are in voluntary thrall to Swamiji the spiritual guide as he creates an illusion of divinity by singing Rama-Gopala! Hare Krishna! In reality the Swamiji is a knave humbug waiting to victimize these innocent devotees to satiate his fleshly thirst. The foolish devotion of three girls has been aptly defined by S. Krishnaswamy as:

> They placed their faith in the Swamiji, thinking he will bring succour to their tormented souls and transform them into new unified beings at peace with themselves and the world. Instead we have a sordid picture of selfish manipulation, social abuse, midnight orgies and callousness verging on cruelty. The Swamiji treats them as his possessions....[10]

This bogus and sinister godman is a master manipulator. Apart from sexual lust he also has another hidden aim to go abroad for a lecture to hypnotize the people there with his spell-binding hypocrisy. He is so cunning in his dealing with these credulous expatriate women that all the three are subtly jealous of each other for the privilege of serving Swamiji. Evie is his silent, obedient slave: in the manner of a pimp, he has already seasoned her, already broken her in. About his next victim Lee, he explains to Raymond: "I want her to be mine. She must be mine completely in heart and soul and—yes, Raymond; he said, easily able to read his companion's thoughts, in body also, if I think it necessary."[11]

In her quest to become a new person Lee, in a hypnotized state of mind, walks into the Swamiji's hut at midnight and undergoes a traumatic experience of rape. The tormented girl narrates the trauma of this rape. "He was terrible, terrifying, he drove right on into me and through me and calling me beastly names, shouting them out loud and at the same time hurting me as much as he could" (*A New Dominion*, p. 199).

Lee's sexual harassment by the Swamiji at midnight is frightening at any standard. After facing this self-destruction Lee's scorn and disgust for her fanatic endeavours of spiritualism is intensely pathetic. Swamiji is a rogue and such hypocrites have brought ignominy to Indian spiritual heritage abroad. They deserve hellish treatment here and in public. Truly speaking, no punishment can be called too severe for them. Kavita Sharma passes the sentence: "There is no room for forgiveness in these god-men's ruthless betrayal of the softest and highest emotions of men and women looking for spiritual rejuvenation."[12]

But it is strange that Lee has reached the point of no return in her relation with the Swamiji who has no qualms, either moral or religious in abusing her. Though she once breaks out of his magnetic spell and runs under the protective umbrella of rationalistic westerners like Raymond and Mrs. Charlotte, yet her escape is all too brief and in spite of her brutal rape at Swamiji's hands she again returns to his Ashram. Lee's predicament, even at the end of the novel, implicit in her incapability to distinguish between simple bodily pleasures and spiritual bliss, remains as puzzling as ever.

This oddity of *A New Dominion* stems from curious authorial tendency to state everything in duplicate or triplicate. For instance, we discover not just one Lee but at least two additional versions of her in the characters of Evie and Margaret, the identical characters whose differences lie mainly in terms of their degrees of commitment to the Swamiji. Margaret has rather a deep faith in Swamiji's spiritual powers—deeper even than Lee's because when she contracts infections and deadly diseases hepatitis and jaundice she does not admit it. She has lost all her rationality under the spell of Swamiji's mysterious wisdom and spirituality. Margaret's will is broken because her health fails her. However, she pins her faith on the holy man's powers of rejuvenation and, though on the verge of death, she rejects Raymond's advice and offer of hospitalization and treatment at all.

This Swamiji dupes Margaret and consequently she dies a miserable death as a mindless stupor in the dominion of Swami. Obviously the quests of these British girls end in self-delusion and self-destruction. Pertinently Lourie Sucher observes:

> That is the outcome of the ashram story in the novel; the danger that Margaret, Lee, and Evie flirt with is finally, death. It may appear to be spiritual commitment, it may appear to be sexual love: in either case, its point of utmost intensity, its logical extreme, is annihilation.[13]

Besides the spiritual dominion Jhabvala also projects the new complex of East-West interaction on individual level. The assertion of a new dominion takes place at many levels but most strikingly in its effect on the sensibility of westerners vis-a-vis sensuality of Indians. Mrs. Jhabvala, taking the position of an expatriate woman writer, articulates these experiences of westerners with the ironic vision of a social realist. The general mentality of Indians is exposed in Gopi's character who establishes friendship with Lee only to compel her to surrender to his sexuality. In exhorting Lee he expresses his perverted attitude towards all the western women:

> Everyone knew that western girls were brought up on sex, lived on sex. She must have slept with many many men over and over again. This thought suddenly excited and infuriated him. (*A New Dominion*, pp. 53-54)

Gopi is a representative of oriental sexuality and urges Lee for sexual intercourse. When she innocently expresses her unwillingness for physical contact by saying she never thought of it, Gopi rebukes her: "Never thought of it: As if you English and American girls ever think of anything else! Everyone knows it" (*A New Dominion*, p. 54).

Finding it impossible to make him understand herself by means of words, Lee surrendered her body. She suffered rather than enjoyed while doing this for him but was glad for his sake. Raymond is another lover of Gopi whose experiences are parallel to those of Lee's. Like Lee's obsessive love for Swamiji, in rivalry to two other girls Raymond also has a rival—Asha, who ultimately succeeds in snatching Gopi from him. Asha, the pervert young princess, is nymphomaniac and a pretentious exploiter of males like Gopi and even Raymond. Her problem is once again 'existential' in nature; she is worried about the passing of time, about ageing and loss of power particularly over men.

Thus, Jhabvala exposes the moral degradation, hypocrisy and sexuality of Indians like Swamiji, Gopi and Asha who exploit the western seekers aiming at attaining the Indian glory. The novel primarily projects the basic irony that in search of these British girls for spiritual India they find themselves in a personal predicament of hellishness just opposite to their romantic expectations. V.A. Shahane is right in his assessment of *A New Dominion*:

> The Indians in this novel are almost invariably sensual, sex hungry, hypocritical, pretentious, egoistitic and self willed except for Banubai, the puzzling prophetess, and Bob, a go ahead young man.[14]

Thus, the morality is at its lowest ebb in the country as the novel is not merely of a few individuals thrown together but of a country in a moment of meeting of two different cultures. It fails to solve the enigma of failure of three women's attempt to build a bridge between the two extremes.

Heat and Dust which brought the Booker Prize for Ruth Jhabvala in 1975, the year of its publication, was something of a watershed for this expatriate novelist. This most celebrated novel came at the end of a series of three novels which dwell upon the dilemma of western women living in India. More strikingly after this novel Jhabvala took her final flight for the United States after living in India for 25 years of her married life. *Heat and Dust* is again a sordid tale of misadventures of the Europeans coming to India either on administrative task or for spiritual enlightenment or on some other adventurous mission. Jhabvala presents the European individuals especially women suffering from the agony of a tragic obsession with India—the country that metamorphoses every being and everything.

What strikes at the outset is the effect of the Indian environment on the Europeans' sensibilities, particularly on those of women. "India always changes people and I have been no exception"[15] with these emphatic words the narrator of Ruth Jhabvala's most celebrated novel initiates the moving study of the theme which has been at the heart of all these novels of Indo-European phase. It is a double-layered novel portraying the fortunes of two English women (Olivia and her step-granddaughter the Narrator) with a gap of fifty years in imperial and independent India. The story is again told from a woman's point of view as it delineates the fatal consequences of the religious, erotic and the sentimental embrace of India by western women.[16]

A unique thing about this most appreciated novel is that Jhabvala makes extensive and successful use of interior monologue, journals and letters. The novel is the best example of Jhabvala's most characteristic technique—cinematic flashback, using a combination of first and third person narrative; and the themes—the dangers of sexual passions and involvements for western women in India. The sensibilities and fortunes of two expatriate women are contrasted when a young hippy-like girl of 1973, embracing both India and Indian lover, immerses herself in the journal kept by her grandfather's unfaithful wife in India of 1923. The two plots echo and overlap each other, which enable us to see Olivia in the girl and the girl herself as a second Olivia.

The two heroines—Olivia a romantic idealist and the Narrator an anti-romantic modern observer—are in close interaction with India and Indians and in this way portray the drama of East-West malaise with a gap of half a century. The young Narrator comes here to probe and solve the enigma of her step-grandmother's elopement scandal with an Indian Nawab of Khatm but ironically she herself succumbs to her Indian lover under identical conditions and becomes junior Olivia.

Olivia comes on scene as a beautiful, bored and wilful girl of pre-independence ruling English gentry. It is curious how this newly wed wife of the district collector Mr. Douglas—a man of power, authority and her native identity—falls for a second man of same built but somehow opposite of Douglas's staunch Englishness. Whereas Douglas represents the colonial values of British Empire, the Nawab represents undisguised contempt towards all that is English. As a young bride Olivia adored Douglas River's gentlemanly idealism but with the passage of time and the closer perspective of wifehood, her ardour fades and India, as always, makes overwhelming demands on her. Despite Douglas's insistence that the Nawab is the worst type of ruler—the worst type of Indian—you can have, a dacoit's chief—the Nawab remains as irresistible a force of attraction for Olivia as the Swamiji is to Lee in *A New Dominion*. When Harry explains Nawab as a very strong, very manly person Olivia pins her instinct in him. Reacting against her cold husband, though an efficient and stern administrator, Olivia chooses to become the beloved of the corrupt, childish, homosexual but attractive Nawab linked to the lineage of Mughals displaced by the British. Analysing the cause of Olivia's scandalous affair Ronald Shepherd states: "Olivia's urges seem nothing less than her desire to be dominated by a strong man who possesses all the strength, authority and control lacking in her own life."[17]

Olivia is trapped in the bungalow on hot summer afternoons behind closed-down windows and reminds us of the similar scenes in other novels of Jhabvala as well as her dramatization of herself in *Myself in India*. The Nawab is a man who appears the promising oasis for Olivia to come out of stagnant boredom in British aristocracy. He and Olivia recognize in each other a kindred spirit and a mutual need in order to explore some romantic possibility which is needed to push off the drabness of the ordinary world. For Olivia this romance necessitates a sloughing of Englishness in favour of some new identity. This 'pushing off and crossing over' is driven by a more obsessional personal need—not just a testing of water but a grim determination from the very start to ensure total immersion even at the risk of drowning.

Moreover, it is not only Nawab but also the cultural and religious heritage of this primitive land that starts looking illusionary and honourable to Olivia. For instance, when major Minnies, Douglas and Dr. Saunders discuss and criticise the hair-raising events of suttee Olivia resents being spared and argues that it is old cultural beauty and grace of India.

Olivia, contrary to her European sensibility, takes the most romantic view of the widow's self-sacrifice thinking it noble to want to go with the person she cares for most in the world. It indicates that Olivia has undergone the complete process of metamorphosis that India causes to its foreign visitors. Despite her sensitivity, intelligence and awareness of Indian cultural matters, she remains totally at sea in matters regarding her own emotions and desires and never attempts to rationalize her feelings towards Nawab and his crude culture.

The feeling of personal entrapment, the fear of losing her precarious mental balance, the fear (as with Asha in *A New Dominion*) of growing old and ordinary, the fear of being a loser in the game of passion—all these things constitute a state of mind that compels Olivia to revolt. Consequently, Olivia of Satipur allows herself to be drawn into a liaison with the quixotic, unrealistic, crude and sensual Nawab of Khatm (the Hindi word that means finished). It is pathetic that the erotic obsession that Olivia thinks love is her victimization at the hands of this insensitive and dubious Nawab who uses her to felicitate his political and sexual ends either for 'revenge' or as a 'spy' against the British Empire. Like others of Ruth Jhabvala's bored and lovely women Olivia also risked her all for love and like them also ran off with her demon-lover, who is obsessively exciting and dangerous.

The Nawab finds opportunity to allure Olivia to Baba Firdaus's fertility shrine where barren women go with a faith to get blessings for a son and heir. Arousing the emotions of credulous Olivia, Nawab seduces her. The scene of seduction at the holy shrine is in itself weird, and taxes one's credibility. But more treacherous than this is the insensitivity of the Nawab towards his daring beloved when Olivia becomes pregnant probably with his child. Poor Olivia does not realise that she has become pregnant at a wrong time by a wrong man and in a wrong way. It is disgusting on Nawab's part that in place of bestowing his protective affection on the wretched woman he advises her to abort the child. Accordingly, the Indian midwives perform an abortion but a straitlaced British physician whom Olivia, of course knows socially discovers it. Being 'ruined' she flees to the Nawab's palace from where she is probably made to leave for a secluded place in the Himalayas to live out a solitary life there as her penance.

Hence, she is compelled to leave a less than perfect marriage with her demon-lover. Her final motivation to turn her back on human society at all remains obscure despite all researches of the Narrator. The novelist has presented the transformation of the romantic heroine Olivia, a naive and innocent victim; as the modern Narrator creates her we come to accept her as a beatified foremother. The Nawab is a further enhancement in the series of obsessive demon-lovers of western women in Jhabvala's India of charismatic Swamiji of *A New Dominion*. The best assessment of Nawab is explicit in his symbolic fiefdom Khatm meaning 'finished' as his spell of attraction leads his innocent beloved from self-delusion to self-destruction. With a rare critical probe Lourie Sucher brings out this purpose of Jhabvala. Her words deserve quoting:

> The Nawab's creator herself is characteristically ambivalent towards him. He is one of a long line of charismatic, seductive men in her fiction who, while they can not be trusted, represent vitality, intelligence and a certain very welcome force of opposition to the hypocritical and suffocating dullness of the world in which female protagonist finds herself.[13]

The young detective Narrator is the product of the permissive but skeptic western breed who comes to India where the British no longer hold sway. She is the granddaughter of Douglas from his second wife whom he married after the doom of Olivia. She belongs to the new generation of liberal-minded and well-educated women of refined sense and sensibilities from Europe and she makes a journey of India to solve the enigma of Olivia's scandal. The entire substance of the novel is filtered through the consciousness of the Narrator who becomes both the instrument and the subject of her creator's ironic view of life.

The Narrator actually competes with the nominal heroine Olivia and the readers' interest even turns out to be more in this younger heroine out of the two. Olivia, after all, stands at some historical distance away and our knowledge of her depends wholly on Narrator's interpretation; whereas the Narrator is herself closer to us, the possessor of a strange mixture of calm intelligence and intractable obsession. In spite of some elaborate parallels that exist between these two central women of *Heat and Dust*, it is the difference between them that is more significant and conspicuous from the feminist point of view.

The modern Narrator also takes freedom of movement and even sexual freedom as she is on a tour of this country without any protective umbrella of her European community as was in case of Olivia. But she is more cautious; her emotional detachment is the polar opposite of Olivia's passionate abundance. Throughout the novel the modern Narrator resists the shocked voices that predict danger of her; in a stance of stubborn, almost ostentatious, carelessness, she goes wherever she pleases. After the telescoped plot synopsis, the Narrator quotes a passage from her own journal describing her arrival in Bombay.

The Narrator's first act on arrival is to head for the dormitory of the S.M. Hostel, Society for Missionaries, she supplies in a parenthesis. One must wonder whether Ruth Jhabvala has intended the sly pun. Can anyone hear the initial S.M. without thinking of the 'erotic minority'—Sadomasochism: whether the association is intentional or not there are certainly links. This novel, like virtually all of Ruth Jhabvala's works, touches on the commonalities between obsessional religious devotion and obsessional romanticism. At any rate, having arrived at the hostel, the Narrator puts her watch on top of her suitcase and falls into an exhausted sleep. Awakening in darkness, she gropes for her watch, finds it missing, and is already lamenting its loss when a voice from the next bed admonishes her tartly: "Here it is, my dear, and just be more careful in future, please" (*Heat and Dust*, p. 3). The disembodied voice belongs to a Christian missionary who for thirty years has been tending the souls of poor Indians. Now she attends to her compatriot with advice and warnings. Wearing a white nightgown that encases her from head to foot, she is compared several times to a ghost. Indeed, she points out to the Narrator very much in the fashion of a Dantean angel, the various rings of inferno that can be seen from their windows in the S.M.: the Indian street seen below bright as day with naptha flares though it is half-past midnight, crowded with the wretched, crippled children, a legless boy, scavengers of the leavings of hawkers of food and their customers. If the wretched Indians seem light hearted the privileged European vacationers in India are wretched as we, along with the Narrator, see through the window of S.M. Hostel: a crowd of derelict Europeans mostly young.

The ghostly guide demands rhetorically—"Who are they, where do they come from?" (*Heat and Dust*, p. 5) and then relates the miserable plight of a young German or Scandinavian whom she has seen being deloused, in the street by a monkey. Looking into his face, the missionary sees 'a soul in hell' and the Narrator concurs: "The hippies across the way look to her too like souls in hell" (*Heat and Dust*, p. 6). The elderly missionary has symbolically warned the Narrator's consciousness of a risk in the land of her arrival, but modern Narrator blithely ignores. There is much to fear in this India which once had devoured her step-grandmother Olivia and now has so reduced her compatriots.

As in all other novels of Jhabvala it is ironical that all warning voice of European rationalism and Christian ethos falls on deaf ears in the same way as major Minnies' theories of the horror of the influence of India on European temperament had not brought any rationality to Olivia. The young Narrator drowns herself in this pit of self-delusion in India. A thematic verbal motif emerges here, i.e. a play with images of standing up or lying down, resisting or submitting to the seduction of India; a name that can represent sensuality, chaos, and the non-rational.

Therefore, it is the re-cycling retreat of history that the Narrator also, even more than Olivia's fall and submission to the Nawab, surrenders herself to an ordinary worthless clerk under identical conditions. The young Narrator, who is already frayed by India's poverty, could not resist herself from becoming a plaything for sensual Inder Lal in whose house she is a co-tenant. In this unpredictable embrace of their Indian lovers Olivia and the Narrator are neatly sliced two halves of a single personality. It is surprising that the young Narrator, seeking to reconstruct Olivia's life in India, should in an identical circumstance get pregnant in spite of all her self-restraints. It is the same fertility shrine of Baba Firdaus and the same celebration of the Husband's wedding day on which the Nawab made Olivia pregnant. More than this, as if to add a positive implication, where as Olivia's fate was negative one—a squalid abortion—the Narrator decides to have her child by an Indian father. Ruth Jhabvala seems to hint at this strengthening and progressive change in the sensibilities of European women after a gap of half a century in Indian context. David Rubin's words are worth quoting:

> Olivia aborted her half-Indian baby but remains faithful to his Indian father, whereas the narrator in a more enlightened age, or perhaps merely one more decadent, though she discards her Indian lover after unsuccessfully trying to abort her child, finds a rapture in the idea of having it.[19]

There is a double irony here for the detached Narrator, on a quest to solve the enigma of Olivia's scandal, she herself becomes a victim of same scandal and moves towards the isolation in hills and will herself seek remedy in pilgrimage. The most strange and intractable mystery of the novel becomes not what happened to self-deluded Olivia, but rather how to account for this sensible modern young woman's willing obsession and submission to Indian demands and illusions which, she already knew, are fatal in consequences. Yasmine Goonaratne highlights the Narrator's self-imposed isolation: "Her impulse to increased self-isolation in order to find spiritual fulfillment combines with her tendency to idealise Olivia's vision to suggest a growing psychological imbalance."[20]

More mystifying than previous novels of Ruth Jhabvala is the choice of these two disintegrated and distorted women to go in exile. Jhabvala's earlier women characters have two well-defined options before them after they have experienced the vicious circle of living in India: either to fly back to Europe to survive and revive their shattered sensibilities or to succumb to the obsessive forces in India and face self-destruction, e.g. Lee in *A New Dominion* and Judy in *A Backward Place*. But in this novel Jhabvala makes both of her heroines stay in this country although in a half-hearted manner. They do not stay with their obsessive lovers but they are sent to mountains away from the heat and stench, dust and squalor that constitutes an important part of the reality of India in the corpus of Jhabvala's novels. It is really thrilling though tragic when we see the pregnant young woman—the Narrator—madly possessed with the romantic impulse, climbing higher and higher and never to look down any more. The novel stops short before the Narrator sets out on the next stage of her 'quest' and we are left to speculate about the inevitable self-destruction or unpredictable heroism declaring some victory of femininity over masculinity in this final ascent. If so then certainly the mountains symbolize feminine power and the hot perched Indian Plains the masculine domain and the growing child in the Narrator's womb—the final trophy of this East-West encounter. However, if the author hopes the birth of this child to be a symbol of new life, of some new harmonious beginning amidst the arid, dry ruins encountered so far, it is a slim hope indeed. The world here is as unready to welcome an offspring of doubtful and irreconcilable parentage and its breeding mother as was in India of Olivia's time.

As this study is more centered on a feminine approach to the options available to the women searchers seeking wholeness, exaltation and comprehending transcendence, these are the qualities that convention and society seems to deny them. Both the women, in spite of all their sincere quest for some transcendental realisation, are enthralled by masculine authority not only in their desires for love but also in the prospects of some erotic transcendental power. In this respect there is an uneasy combination of the sacred and the profane, the spiritual and the sexual and the normal and perverse in the erotic and sexual intrigues of the novel. The easy fall of two women at distant times to the call of flesh at holy shrine of Baba Firdaus may be ascribed to the powers of saint enshrined in the tomb. Similarly, the young Narrator succumbs to the sexual demands of an ascetic from Europe renamed Chidanand who wrongly thinks himself living on a higher plane of Indian spiritualism. The Narrator realises the hellish predicament of this damned soul who boasts of himself as a purified Hindu but is actually on the way of self-destruction and death. The Narrator rescues him and provides food and shelter in her room. But on recovering from illness this converted Chid is too demanding on her and not only for food but he also needs sex very badly. The sexual ride by Chid makes her think of a possible spiritual emanation from some power outside himself.

Jhabvala is very sarcastic and rather intentionally biased in making the Narrator describe Chid's erection with the dexterity of a piousness for Hindu god Shiva:

> But he has constant erections and goes to a tremendous size so that I am reminded of the Lord Shiva whose huge member is worshipped by devout Hindu women. At such times it seems to me that his sex is engendered by his spiritual practices, by all that chanting of mantras he does sitting beads in hand on the floor of my room. (*Heat and Dust*, p. 65)

Thus, Jhabvala investigates the combination of spiritual longing and erotic obsession that her characters know as love or a spiritual call. The novel focuses on an English woman's infatuation with the Nawab—the 20th century royal but selfish and dubious lover. On the other side, her granddaughter, with no infatuation, submits to erotic and fleshly calls of a worthless clerk and to a derelict European ascetic facing hellish predicament in India. Here is found Ruth Jhabvala's most pointed deconstruction of the Gothic-romantic adventures especially as it applies to the western women in India. The two intertwined stories continue the exploration of the links between romance and pornography: they are 'passion' and 'desecration' the latter especially.

Thus, these novels of Indo-European interactions are focused on the expatriate women in their search for love, beauty and spirituality in varying degrees and Jhabvala articulates how their search backfires and destroys these women in India. The infatuating and illusionary love affairs, troubled marriages between European women and Indian men; the romantic quest of the vague and credulous self-seekers from the west; their misadventures, boredom, friction and disintegration or flight for survival are depicted through so many female protagonists from the western countries transplanted in Indian society. This East-West awareness leading to conflict is exposed mainly on three levels: (a) the incompatibility of personal sensibility and circumstantial realities; (b) the incongruities consequent upon inharmonious blending of two modes of life—the Eastern and the Western; and (c) the predicament of illusion-bound women facing tragic disintegration of their personality and identity or survival by flight from this subcontinent of weird culture.

Consensus appears to be that *A Backward Place* marks a shift in Jhabvala's oeuvre from a sympathetic mockery of the comic humane to a darker, more scaring vision of life in urban India which continues in the next two novels. Paul Sharrad has rightly observed this change as:

> In this latter phase, the negative treatment of India is highlighted and this prejudices Jhabvala's readership in two ways: she is castigated for reproducing colonialist patterns of presentation and also for touting a biased expatriate European view of a limited section of Indian society.[21]

To say, while Jhabvala's earlier novels like those of any genuine Indian writer, tend to deal with Indians as people first and only secondarily as Indians, here in the Indo-European saga this order is reversed as the westerners are in India to experience the Indian life on their pulse. In this phase Jhabvala's attitude has sharpened and her craftsmanship has sufficiently matured as she sarcastically highlights the various points of clash and conflict between the characters from two uncompromising socio-cultural backgrounds. A subtle somewhat ironical and feminine twist is given to the hackneyed, everlastingly interesting theme of the East-West encounter.

Though Jhabvala's locale is still Delhi—the city of old traditional subcontinent in microcosm and the reader is expected to be a European or at least one having European awareness and sensibility, she, with a matured vision, articulates the demon-like metamorphic effects of India on illusionary westerners especially women. Nevertheless this predicament of European women does not invalidate the romantic quest itself as the errant female protagonists learn by shedding naive-illusions about man, romance, sex and religion. Their experiences yield neither cynicism nor even renunciation but only deeper curiosity which will persist with a much more morbid exposure in Jhabvala's novels written in United States after leaving India.

NOTES

1. Ruth Prawer Jhabvala, quoted in *Contemporary Novelist* (New York: St. Martin's Press, 1976), p. 270.
2. David Rubin, "Ruth Jhabvala in India", *Modern Fiction Studies*, Vol. 30, No. 4 (West Lafyette: Perdue Unit Winter, 1984), p. 674.
3. Ruth Prawer Jhabvala, *A Backward Place* (Delhi: Hind Pocket Books, 1965), p. 5.
4. Hayden M. Williams, appraisal of Judy is worth quoting as: "The most successful surrender to India is that of Judy, an English woman married to vain Indian actor with illusions of grandeur and aspirations beyond his limited talents, a restless and unhappy would be film star who frightens Judy by his determination to leave the large warm extended family in Delhi for the risky life in the fiercely competitive Bombay film industry." "A Retrospective Look at Ruth Prawer Jhabvala's Career as a Novelist: The Indian Novels", *Passage to Ruth Prawer Jhabvala*, ed. Ralph J. Crane (New Delhi, 1991), p. 8.
5. C. Saros and V.A. Shahane, *Modern Indian Fiction* (Delhi: Vikas Publishing House Pvt. Ltd., 1965), p. 44.
6. *cf.* Ronald Shepherd also perceives Jhabvala's own face in these three women from Europe, "More specifically, these three women at the centre of *A Backward Place* dramatise Jhabvala's own difficulty not just with India but with herself. At the centre of this novel there is an existential dilemma, arising from an uncertain authorial identity." *Jhabvala in India: The Jewish Connection* (Delhi: Chanakya Publication, 1994), p. 100.
7. V.A. Shahane, *Ruth Prawer Jhabvala* (New Delhi: Arnold Heinmann Publishers Pvt. Ltd., 1976), p. 78.
8. V.A. Shahane, "Ruth Prawer Jhabvala's *A New Dominion*", *The Journal of Commonwealth Literature*, Vol. XII, No. 1, August (1977), p. 6.
9. *Ibid.*, p. 47.

10. Shanta Krishnaswamy, *White Woman's Burden: The Women in Indian Fiction in English (1950-80)* (New Delhi: Ashish Publishing House, 1984), p. 325.
11. Ruth Prawer Jhabvala, *A New Dominion* (London: Granada Publishing Ltd., 1983), p. 146.
12. Kavita A. Sharma, "Jhabvala on Godmen", *The Radical Humanist*, Vol. 43, No. 8, Nov. 1979, p. 34.
13. Lourie Sucher, *The Fiction of Ruth Prawer Jhabvala: The Politics of Passion* (London: The Macmillan Press Ltd., 1989), p. 57.
14. V.A. Shahane, "Ruth Prawer Jhabvala's *A New Dominion*", *op. cit.*, p. 52.
15. Ruth Prawer Jhabvala, *Heat and Dust* (London: Futura Publications. A Division of Macdonald & Co. Publishers Ltd., 1993), p. 1.
16. *cf.* Lourie Sucher: "In *Heat and Dust* the story is told from a woman's perspective, with an emphasis on women's options, women's expectations and women's solutions", *op. cit.*, p. 102.
17. Ronald Shepherd, *Jhabvala in India: The Jewish Connection* (Delhi: Chanakya Publication, 1994), p. 132.
18. Lourie Sucher, *op. cit.,* p. 110.
19. David Rubin, *op. cit.*, p. 661.
20. Yasmine Goonaratne, *op. cit.*, p. 226.
21. Paul Sharrad, "Passing Moments: Irony, Ambivalence and Time in A Backward Place", *Passages to Ruth Prawer Jhabvala*, ed. Ralph J. Crane (New Delhi: Sterling Publishers Pvt. Ltd., 1991), p. 37.

5

Final Phase: Women in the Cross-cultural Amalgam of the American Milieu

The literary career of Ruth Jhabvala entered in its final phase with her shifting from India to the United States in 1975. In this new move towards west her focus has widened to the cosmopolitan dimension as she portrays the woman's point of view regarding the complex manifestations of feminine sensibilities in this saga of human relations. Her women protagonists and even other women characters, in spite of all their freedom of life, suffer from obsessive and paradoxical compulsions of love and unscrupulous infatuations, which are strangely out of their control. As the following account will show, Jhabvala in this phase exposes the clash of generations in this setting of racial admixture and multi-cultural confluence with all its bleak ramifications on the sensibilities of womenfolk at large. There is a strange labyrinth of undefined relationships in these American novels and the milieu is much more disgusting and pessimistic than that of her India-based novels. The institutions of 'home', 'marriage' and 'family' have already collapsed and the characters especially women of mixed race, mixed sexuality and mixed culture reflect this fragmented image as they desperately strive for authenticity, connectedness and spiritual transcendence.

In Search of Love and Beauty (1983) marks this audacious departure of this expatriate woman towards her closer roots that she finds in America due to the racial tragedies of twentieth century history. Although every woman in Jhabvala's fictional world has been in search of love and beauty, this novel examines this feminine search on a group of German and Austrian refugees and two generations of their descendants in New York. Ruth Jhabvala, herself a displaced central-European Jew, has, perhaps, given an autobiographical touch to the story by fitting it in this city of European refugees and thus opening the door into her ancestral past. Due to the obvious influence of her screenplay profession, the novelist now incorporates flashback filmic technique as the novel juxtaposes events happening over a span of sixty years and the reader is plunged into crucial moments throughout the course of three generations. The novel is an attempt to probe into the malaise of a hopeless and hapless overriding obsession which drives all before it and is some how transmitted through generations whether in spirituality seekers group or between lovers—both heterosexuals and homosexuals.

Lousie and Regi are girlhood friends in a suburb of Germany. At eighteen Lousie is courted by Bruno Sonnenblick, a sensitive and poetic Jew of thirty-six. He is an idealist but his idealism is betrayed by Lousie in spite of his adoration of her as his goddess. Even after their move to New York in the thirties—the dreadful reason for which is not explicitly mentioned—these refugee women are now more close and physically intimate friends. They lead a luxurious life but still suffer from a sense of meaninglessness and boredom as agonizing as experiencing death-in-life. Finding their lesbian affinity incompetent they are linked with a dubious and charismatic guru Leo who has a wonderful gift of looking into the inner beings of women and thus tracing their secret longings and desires. Both the women feel a necessity to put themselves into his hands as they have "Proliferated into such a complicated personality that they can no longer manage themselves and must hand themselves over to someone else, someone stronger" (*In Search of Love and Beauty*, p. 37). This charlatan genius is founder of his dubious 'Academy of Potential Development'. Leo soon becomes irresistible to

Lousie, even against her will just as the Swamiji had become for Lee in *A New Dominion.* When Lousie and Bruno's daughter Marietta are still child Leo overtakes this family as he moves with Lousie in their apartment. Bruno suffers stoically and with this self-delusion of three generations is already initiated which the novelist picturises through a rich mosaic of episodes shifting back and forth from 1930s to the day. The novel reiterates the predicament of naive and wily women in clutches of the dubious guru as linked by the incessant longing for inner fulfilment. Grandmother Lousie, mother Marietta, adopted daughter Natasha and even son Mark pursue their selfish motifs by their different routes. Yet each of them is drawn, either by love or hate to the charismatic guru who, in reality, is an American version of the Swamiji of *A New Dominion.* It is noteworthy that Jhabvala here presents a dubious guru who is not Indian but a westerner. Leo is a Jew, an artist who has won over so many followers especially women by dint of his fraudulent practice of synthesis of psychiatry, theatrical technique and oriental spirituality. Its premise is reported as early as the first line of the novel: "Everyone always knew that Leo Kellermann had something, was someone special."[1]

The shocking event of the novel is the ousting of gentleman Bruno by sexually dominant Leo in their tussle for dominance on Lousie. It is pathetic that Bruno, the Jew representing impotency goes down without a whimper silently ascending to Leo—symbolizing lion—representing the fascist virility and triumphal takeover of his wife. Marietta grows to hate her mother Lousie's lover who has been trying to molest this innocent girl also since her childhood.

Bruno, a cautious father, has always made efforts to safeguard his daughter against such traumatic realities. However, Marietta being well aware of this sexual intimacy between her mother and the fascist male intruder in their house, had been angrily shouting at her mother for her submission to this manipulator—psychological as well as sexual. A Gothic scene of sexual orgy between Leo and Lousie, accidentally and unfortunately witnessed by innocent Marietta, causes a psychological havoc and disturbance to the infant sensibility of this girl.

Marietta says nothing about it, though she wonders mightily at its meaning and at the meaning of her mother's exclamation "I'm coming." Her molestation at Leo's hand and this hunting scene with her mother develops contempt towards sex in her except her half-hearted encounter with Ahmad in New York. Although she spends most of her life resentful to Leo, it is strange that in her adult life when Leo thrusts himself sexually upon her she is immensely aroused. At the sixtieth birthday of Lousie, Leo cunningly seduces Marietta who still hates him but it is strange enough that she experiences blissful orgasm which hitherto had eluded her. She is psychologically perturbed but feels an internal urge to relish this intercourse with this powerful male.

To her surprise, Marietta also exclaims 'yes, yes I'm coming' just like her mother at the time of seduction. The comedy becomes sour in taste when daughter so betrays a mother who has already betrayed the father by open intimacy with a charlatan guru. In this wilful sexual encounter with Leo, Marietta exhibits the secret love for her violation in the same way just as Lee is obsessed with devilish Swamiji in *A New Dominion*. Ronald Shepherd seems to endorse this opinion as he comments:

> Here is the victim's misplaced secret love of her violation and violator, the respect of the oppressed for its oppressor which of course also translates into (but really has its' roots in) more political and cultural terms. The overriding obsession in this novel, despite the novel's title, is not so much with love and beauty as with the need to be rescued by male power, to become at one with the male violator. Self-hatred condones the violator's molestation of the self as something deserved. And masochistic self-laceration becomes a necessary rite of passage to discovery and longed for renewal.

Leo's 'Academy for Potential Development' is a sort of western Ashram catering for the psycho-spiritual needs of well-bred but dissatisfied young persons, mostly female. He willingly plays the role of a sadist evident in the angling metaphor of woman as resisting fish in the method of scape goating which is a part of his therapy. He proclaims: "All women are crazy. You have to look out for them" (*In Search of Love and Beauty*, p. 79).

Jhabvala also portrays the emergence of gay rights activism in popular consciousness, which is both a result of the disillusionment with heterosexual romance and the sign of an important social reality in the life of late twentieth century America. Marietta's son Mark fights to takeover the proprietorship of Kent who is a typical hermaphrodite male in physical appearance and female in temperament. The overriding love of Marietta finds bizarre expression when she takes up secretly with Kent. In this sexual relationship between an over-middle aged woman and her son's homosexual lover they are excited strangely by talking about their common love-Mark. Marietta's ambivalent sensation on Kent's remark on her physique similar to her son is quite obscene and incestuous as it "penetrated her as no physical relation of her own ever had done" (*In Search of Love and Beauty*, p. 158).

Similarly, the sexual activities of Jeff and Staphine—the two followers of Leo, are frequently stimulated by the presence of a third person observer in Natasha. Among the homosexuals, woman finds herself alienated from her males as well as from other women. One might logically expect some acknowledgement of the female homosexuality as there are lesbians like Lousie and Regi but this female homosexuality is pathological and comic and no satisfactory option or cementing force among women. Lourie Sucher encapsulates thus:

> By their attention to women's psychology, by their female perspectives and by their inclusion of so many male homosexual characters, her novels and stories push us in the direction of at least noticing the absence of female friendships or love between women.

At the core of this novel there is a female friendship—between tolerant Lousie and bitchy Regi—about which the best that can be said is that with a friendship like that one needs no enemies. There is no reciprocity in their friendship so when even in the final scene of the novel Lousie clings to Regi on the ice, she delivers a characteristic response "Let me go, you stupid goose" and Lousie falls to her death.

One more woman in this novel is Sujata—an Indian, and in delineating this character Jhabvala has dipped her pen in acid irony. Her name derives from Sanskrit word meaning 'nobly born' but it is paradoxical that there is nothing noble in her as she is crazy and nymphomaniac. She survives by having numerous amorous affairs and her problem is an existential one. She raises the crucial questions about sex and incest as:

> ...if it was so wrong to have these feelings, then why were they set? Why did they come to a human being—as suddenly, unexpectedly, irresistibly as those notes of perfection, those high moments of highest art that her grandmother had taught her to lie in wait for? If it was wrong, if it was shameful, then why was it there? And why was it so glorious? (*In Search of Love and Beauty*, p. 86)

We are informed that this sex-hungry Indian nymph dies in an accident with a motorcycle rickshaw with a driver who drove like a crazy man symbolically overriding a crazy woman. Even her friendship with Marietta is short-lived and shallow. Thus, all female friendships are obstructed by jealousy, rivalry and the basic insufficiency of woman for other woman. Males in Jhabvala's world are either both homosexual and uninterested in women like Mark, or heterosexual and still disrespectful to women like Leo. The women are either treated as scapegoats to be sacrificed or men return them with disgust and perplexity in place of love. The strange often bizarre confusion and self-destruction which beset most of the female characters in this novel spring from their self-hatred, and internal fragmented psyche which is an underlying problem and malaise of the modern times.

Three Continents (1987) is the second novel of this phase. It deals with the socio-cultural disintegration, spiritual anemia, self-delusion and destructive sexual obsessions of the people after the holocaust. Here the malaise has become comparatively serious and the infliction has decayed the roots of socio-cultural system of the western world. The traditional centres of civilization have lost their relevance as institutions of 'family', 'marriage', 'home' have already died an un-natural death. The decline of Wishwell family and their disintegration in the stronghold of an Oriental trio of Rawul, Crishi and Renee is portrayed by the author and this victimization of naive twins is expressed from a woman's point of view. Parents and children of Wishwell family are all devoid of feelings for one another.

The twins are sufferers of neglected childhood and this hollowness and emotional vacuum have caused an indefinable malaise. Harriet, in the very beginning of the novel, underlines their predicament of internal disintegration due to the lack of parental care and love. Their parents Manton and Lindsay are referred to, in episode after episode, be occupied with their sensual games of pouting and posing and the children are sufferers of a damaged childhood. The Oriental trio exploits the vulnerable twins by creating a fiend semblance of the substitute family which is the need of these unprotected children of rootless community. The Oriental exploiters through their charismatic mechanism known as *Fourth World Movement* or *Transcendental Internationalism* victimize the vulnerable twins by creating a fiend semblance of the substitute family. Rawal has already assigned himself a fathering role and Crishi becomes Michael's lover and soon Harriet also flares with unreasonable sexuality towards Crishi under the promise of marriage. There is a recklessness in the commitment of twins towards the fraudulent movement and it ultimately leads them to their doom.

Harriet Wishwell and her brother Michael form the kind of binary duo seen so often in the patterning of Jhabvala's stories more like one single person than separate individuals. Harriet as the narrator reveals a good deal about what she really suspects—the sinister trap in which Michael falls and soon she also enters for the sake of her brother. In promise of inner strengthening through spiritual enlightenment the twins are made to surrender their self for the sexual and economic rapacity of this oriental scam. After Harriet's involvement with Crishi, her obsessive sexual hunger for Crishi becomes uncontrollable.[4]

In this dramatization of a fascist male masquerade, with its rhetoric of spiritual liberation and even messianic promises and with its swallowing up of Propinquity, i.e. inheritance, reader hears the ironic inversion of invasive western colonialism in respect of Indians. In *Three Continents*, once again Jhabvala tends to interpret what she depicts as reality, the image that India and all that India stands for—religiosity, spirituality, etc.—is a fraud, a deception, at least, in modern context. This hypocrisy has now crossed the border of subcontinent and has spread a vicious network through alluring and charismatic manipulators in the form of trio's cruel absolutism. The triumvirate of 'Transcontinental Internationalism' consists of: Rawul, a fiftieth, plump and affable decoy; the Rani who half way changes the noble title into Renee and is product of mixed lineage—a German mother and an Afghan father; and Crishi who is also of mixed race as his mother was part English, part Assamese and his father anonymous. The mysterious parentage only attributes to the genial charms of these manipulators and Crishi reigns supreme in trapping heterosexual women through homosexual men all over three continents with the sole motif of chatting up those likely to prove useful.

Now along with Michael, Harriet is also enthralled and included in the nightly nude swims full of sexual orgies and incest. Soon Crishi becomes an irresistible obsession for the twins which Crishi thinks a must to felicitate his insidious design to grab their inherited property. The pornographic narration of animalistic sex on the beach with Crishi is an exposition of the deep obsession in Harriet's psyche.

Sexual urgency for Harriet is the counterpart of an ideological urgency for Michael but at deeper level Michael is also driven by sexual urgency with Crishi. Thus, the relationships of twins are characterized by animal lure and contest for being seduced by a fascist masculinity in Crishi. It is pathetic that in the second part of the novel when Crishi fails to appear in the evenings, Harriet feels herself reduced to something less than human:

> He had aroused me so completely that the sex he gave me—rationed out to me was absolutely essential to me. Deprived of it, I was as if without breath and air. Really sometimes I lay there in such an agony of unfulfilled longing, I was fighting to breathe. I was hardly a person anymore but just this fearful need. (*Three Continents*, p. 162)

In the middle section of the novel the movement moves over to Europe and it is ironically titled "The Family". To underline irony the biological family has already disintegrated and era of parental care has passed long as now Manton is coupled with Barbara, Lindsay with Jean and the twins of damaged childhood are in London under the illusionary semblance of new family formed on the basis of physical needs alone. Now for financing the movement Crishi must marry Harriet and so in an attempt to win over the skeptical Harriet, Rani proceeds to arrange this marriage. But it is a tragic irony that in London the scales begin to fall from Harriet's eyes when she comes to know about Crishi's other 'wives'. Moreover, she is also made to share Crishi on the same bed with Rani who otherwise propagates him as her adopted son. Apart from this she also learns about Crishi's ways of smuggling drugs, his escapades in jail, etc. and now she is worried about Michael who has become a part of this racket. In Rawul's case she meets Bari Rani, his real wife and also his three daughters by her, which was a secret so far.

Paradoxically all these pieces of rational advice fall on deaf ears as Harriet's hunger for sexual gratification provided by Crishi increases enormously and she needs it at any cost. Crishi is certainly not less than an electric shock to her and he has become her obsession deep rooted in her psyche and no other relation—even sexual one as she experiments with Salim—could bring her away from this demon lover. She confesses that her inner urge for Crishi is irresistible even if made to share him with Renee on the same bed. She proclaims: "I realized that my ravenous need was not that of any physical animal for another but for one particular human being—for Crishi, for my husband, whom I loved" (*Three Continents*, p. 168).

It is the mysterious and charismatic impact of Crishi on her that Harriet pays no heed to skeptical calls of her own reason and sane warnings from her blood relations. In fact, her mother, her father and also her step-grandmother Sonya all come over to London to warn and rescue Harriet and Michael from this commitment to self-destruction and self-immolation. They try their best to make them understand how blood should hang together with blood and that the family should return to America but all in vain since it is too late to revive the family that has lost its original base of belongingness and meaning at all. Even when Crishi's hypocrisy is revealed to Harriet, she finds herself unable to resist the obsessive infatuation towards him in the same way as Lee could not separate herself from Swamiji even after her brutal rape in *A New Dominion*. The author depicts the predicament of feminine sensibility in the twin's foolhardy and hopelessly idealistic behaviour and their desire to put themselves at risk, to cast aside past connections, to dare annihilation for the promise of some kind of subsequent transcendence.

The last section of the novel makes an Eastward retreat of the movement to India to the very source of it—in the Rawul's kingdom of Dhoka (the Hindi word ironically meaning fraud, trick). If we think of these three continents in their historical order as sites of old-world civilizations, then the movement of the novel is backward into history and with each move Eastward a layer of knavery is revealed. The India of *Three Continents* is, perhaps, more difficult and teetering on the brink of nightmare than what it is in her earlier novels. The ugly truth of this group to be fully revealed in Dhoka is slightly visible in Delhi where the twins are introduced by Crishi to a rowdy group of Rawul's followers called 'Bhais'. These unemployed and penniless youths recruited from Dhoka openly display weapons and are criminals wanted by the police. Crishi's participation in their eunuch dance on the floor of house meant for transcendental mission shocks and infuriates Michael. His obsessive infatuation towards Crishi and his movement disappears when Crishi refuses to prepare for the conference and his words are disgusting to Michael: "I don't care one fuck for your meeting. Not this much, not one fuck" (*Three Continents*, p. 295).

Michael's eyes are now wide open to the realities of this criminal racket. Though too late to rescue, the change is also visible in Harriet as she gives the reason for the direction she has taken when talking to the catholic priest 'Father Tom'. This man appears to speak down to her from his great heights and Harriet drops her eyes to his white feet in Jesus's sandals. Harriet also confides in Tom the reasons of her commitment to this movement saying: "It's the first real family I've ever had, my own family having split up ages ago" (*Three Continents*, p. 311).

Harriet, in her sincere confession of homelessness and emotional vacuum, is like other protagonists of the American novels of Jhabvala. It is again ironical that Harriet should come face to face with a specifying Christian opposition in shape of Father Tom in India and not in America or in England. Moreover, India is presented in all its usual ambivalence as in Delhi and finally in Dhoka the cage-door swings shut upon the deluded, hapless and besotted Harriet. Michael is murdered with the help of Bhais secretly by Crishi while Harriet sleeps peacefully after having been loved. This rogue even manages to have Michael cremated before Harriet and her step-grandmother could realize that Michael is dead. On her arrival at the ruins of Rawul's palace in Dhoka, Crishi misinforms Harriet that her brother has committed suicide. Again this obsessed girl is made to forge a suicide note in full submission to this demon-lover and also a will signed tearfully to give away her inheritance.

We are puzzled to ascertain after all why Harriet surrenders herself even after a full knowledge and realization of her mistake in being entrapped in this fraudulent scam. She signs away everything for the sake of Crishi in spite of the miserable murder of her twin brother by him. There seems no other sustainable reason except that Crishi has turned her into a woman obsessed with unusual sex-hunger—if not love—

which only Crishi could cater her. Harriet's wandering through the decayed palace at Dhoka in the final pages of the novel, is a pathetic wandering of a tragic heroine through a succession of broken mirrors with her fragmented personality caused by her wily embrace of self-destruction. Here is Harriet's psychological picture along with a fake face of her hermaphrodite brother Michael in her words:

> It was as though I were entering him, becoming him; and that was what I tried to do with my thoughts—to make them Michael's thought: What he would have written. I said that I—that is, I, Michael—was going aware because there was nothing in this world that was good enough for me; that I had tried everything and has looked in every direction and there was just absolutely nothing that came up to my expectations. I said that if once you have these expectations—that is of Beauty, Truth and Justice—then you feel cheated by everything that falls short of them; and everything here—that is, here in this world—does fall short of them. It is all *neti, neti*. (*Three Continents*, p. 383)

This concluding passage states the theme that cchoes throughout Jhabvala's oeuvre: the essentially tragic vulnerability of those women and even feminine males like Michael who dream and are in search of love, beauty and transcendent meanings of their existence. To these tantalizing ideals Jhabvala has added the difficult Hebraic pursuit: social justice is after all the ostensible goal of Rawul's ludicrous 'movement' travesty though it may be. *Three Continents* is again a debate of woman with the self on the nature of passion and experiences of romance. But again, in spite of all the traumatic experiences, Harriet reiterates her willing victimization at the hands of her demon-lover Crishi. Jhabvala seems to indicate that her protagonist, even after all skepticism and excruciation, is afflicted with some undefinable malaise and the enemy of the woman is always internal.

In the concluding lines of the novel Harriet is shown madly in love with her sinister captor whom she herself has called a swine and a rogue. Just observe the irresistible will for self-destruction at the hands of her lover Crishi who satiates her sexual desires in his mysterious ways. The ambivalent appeal that Harriet—even more than her twin brother—now finds in Crishi is unresolved enigma of her sensibilities and what actually Harriet finally believes is also an unresolved puzzle of this novel giving unique interpretation to feminine psyche.

Poet and Dancer published in 1993 is set in Manhattan emigre community in recent past and centres on the deep and dangerous intimacy between women in absence of holding the social institution 'family'. Most strikingly, this novel marks a temporary subordination of the theme of Eastern invasion on precarious West through the sinister oriental religious guru cult, to the predicament of women in the broken families, transient and purposeless marriages and deprived childhood. The anchoring institutions of human society have lost their relevance and a revulsion from a society of easy divorce, frequently changing partners, incestuous involvements and internal fragmentation of feminine psyche comes up as the dominant theme here. The novelist has picturised in this novel a story at once as clear and as hauntingly mysterious as a fairy-tale and it is about the nature of passion, quest for identity and the bonds of attachment that are stronger than reason and even than death. The all pervading presence of the Oriental Swami or the manipulative Indian sinister guru is absent in this novel.

The plot of this novel revolves around two cousins—Lara and Angel and the dangerously obsessive sexuality that develops between the two girls. The sexual hazards of lesbian intimacy overriding the heterosexual masculinity in the lives of the two co-protagonists, are presented with dare and ironic vision of a social realist. In the rootless and essence less social milieu of the American emigre community, these two young girls suffer from a disease of emotional congestion and moral vacuum due to the loss of parental warmth. Angel and Lara are the unfortunate children of the emigre community because their parents have lost all their sense and feelings of marital life and are leading an unbridled sexual life in their own ways. Angel is the daughter of Helena—a decadent of Seigfried family of German refugee and she has already discarded her husband Peter. Similarly, Lara's father Hugo, the real brother of Helena—was married but he never brought his wife home and now leads a life of illicit relations with so many women who themselves are otherwise married. Therefore, the two cousins are unfortunate to have estranged parents and no warmth of family and 'home'. Due to this lack of parental warmth and emotional support, the two cousins establish a deep intimacy with each other on their first meeting which ultimately proves self-destructive to them.

When Hugo brought Lara to Angel's house on one of his chance visits, these two otherwise talented cousins wanted to share everything they possessed. Lara was only seven and Angel was eight but they both were suffering from an emotional suffocation and they found an outlet to flow into each other in the gush of overriding passion:

> "Do you like it?" Lara whispered, squeezing Angel's hand between her thighs. Their hearts were beating together under the bed clothes. Lara was twitching and clinging to Angel, and her own hand was now between Angel's thighs, introducing there the strangest sensation. "Go on like I'm doing." She instructed Angel, her heart beating faster, her thighs squeezing tighter, a muscle throbbing there more urgently; her mouth was wide open, her breath blew hot in Angel's face; she was emitting some strong sounds. Quite abruptly all that activity stopped and she rolled away.[5]

The two deprived children suffer from depression, boredom, ennui and emotional insecurity which results in this destructive lesbian intimacy as a substitute. The marital serenity and filial warmth has evaporated from the new generation of America to which Helena, Hugo, Peter and Lilian (Peter's second wife) belong and they are responsible for the psychic deformities and self-delusive commitment of these neglected children. It is an ironical paradox of the fictional expression that Hugo, the irresponsible father of Lara, is a famous psychiatrist much in demand in America and Europe but his own daughter is a critical patient of psychic disorder. In a half-hearted attempt to give Lara a home base Hugo purchases a large apartment in New York but here Lara's self-hatred and agony of meaninglessness deepens since her father's women friends, who are more or less happily married, come to enjoy him shamelessly in the presence of his daughter. With these involvements of her father, Lara suffers from a guilt of non-entity and unwanted being in her own father's house.

Similarly, Angel is also a victim of damaged childhood as she is an unfortunate off-spring of estranged parents who are leading their lives in their own selfish ways. The self-centred involvement of Helena with a wicked Indian woman Mrs. Arora has weakened the ties of mother-daughter bond and Angel feels herself unwanted by her own mother. Angel expresses her own deprivation of motherly love due to the affinity between Helena and mysterious Indian fortune-teller Mrs. Arora. Jhabvala explains the agony of Angel: "They formed such a picture of friendship and togetherness that Angel's first thought was, well, she's all right now, she doesn't need me anymore" (*Poet and Dancer*, p. 95). The mysterious religiosity of Indians mixed with sexuality is again suggested by Jhabvala in the character of Mrs. Arora who has over-possessed Helena to the extent of Angel's frustration.

Selfish Peter coaxes Angel to take Lara close and within the apartment that he purchases for her but solely with his insidious motif of sexual enjoyment with Lara there. With no heed to the individual integrity and proper upbringing of his daughter, Peter facilitates for his incestuous passion for his niece and thus becomes a rival of his own daughter in snatching Lara from her. Angel is well aware of this intrusion in her domain of Lara's love.

Self-dramatizing and self-destructive Lara, embarks upon a love affair with her cousin Angel and her father Peter Keoing simultaneously. Angel is furious at this new affair between Peter and Lara as she does not want to share her beloved with anyone and most objectionably with her own father. On the other side, Lara's sexual urgency is wildly aroused after her indulgence with Peter and she goes neurotic and desperate nymphomaniac and searches relief from depressions through sexuality but with no gain. Jhabvala presents this triangle of incestuous sexual battle in which male overrides female thus:

> Of course Peter came whenever he could entering with an air of absolute possessiveness—which was his right, since he paid the hotel bills. When he arrived, Angel left quickly, although he pretended he wanted her to stay; but Lara took it for granted that it was time for Angel to go. (*Poet and Dancer*, p. 83)

Peter is also afraid of Lara's turning elsewhere for sexual hunger if he fails her and truly when he and Angel both go out, even for their routine works, Lara invites Roland or some other waiter to gratify her sex hunger. It is pathetic that more she indulges more her sexual urgency is aggravated and more neurotic distortion overtakes her sensibilities. In this wild behaviour of father, daughter and a niece in grappling for sexuality, Jhabvala picturises the utter degradation and disintegration of social ethics. When Helena is told about this nefarious act of Peter by Hugo, she bursts with anger on Angel shouting whether her father has gone mad. But it is too late to improve the psychic disorder of Angel and Lara. The novelist ironically lashes at the selfish and careless parents and makes them realise the seriousness of the inner sickness of their deprived children who now do not understand any plea of filial ties. Here life has actually gone out of gear and Lara has become a case of abnormal sexuality whereas Angel has become a parasite on Lara and feeds on her love even if it is rationed to her as a less potent stakeholder. Lara has gone mad with her sexual-hunger and is reduced to a miserable and desperate nymph. When Angel scolds her for her sexual encounter with a receptionist, Lara explains in a confessional tone:

> What else can I do? I'me bored out of my mind all day and he wanted to come up. And I like him; he's nice; he has got a terrific physique—don't you think? Angel? oh! But you wouldn't know about anything like that, would you? (*Poet and Dancer*, p. 158)

So bitchy Lara is bisexual, tolerant Angel is homosexual and in this struggle for sexual bait womanhood is presented at its lowest ebb and in most perverted form. Here we also observe an incestuous rivalry between Peter and his own daughter for sexual possession of a close relative. The spoiled parents could realise the seriousness of the damage caused to their posterity due to their own selfish and perverted involvements and carelessness towards their children. Helena speaks about her daughter's predicament: "She had so utterly given herself to one person that everything else, the whole world, all of us—her own self—everything was dead for her" (*Poet and Dancer*, p. 173).

Thus, Lara, once a romantic and talented girl, is isolated and exploited by this demon and is doomed to self-destruction. Jhabvala narrates the insanity and craziness that has taken over Lara's temperament:

> She knew how unpredictable was her next mood, the next beat of her blood. It wasn't only the danger from outside—that someone might say or do something to disturb her—but the malfunction within her that could suddenly throw her out of gear. (*Poet and Dancer*, p. 180)

It has gone to the offensive attempts by Lara to strangulate her exploiter Peter with her own hands while returning from station by car. Soon after she tries to strangulate Angel and then cuts her own wrist with a razor under a tragic fit of depression. When Angel tries to ask why she has done all this, Lara's answer is full of the existential agony of a woman's loss of faith and experiencing morbid predicament of death-in-life. "Because I don't want to live any more." Jhabvala puts this morbidity entering into Angel's psyche also:

> These hollow words, and the hollow tone in which she spoke them, sank without hindrance to the depth of Angel's soul. The dank sound they made was echoed there. Angel realized that what had once been full was now emptied—the clear running waters of life in which the sky and green leaves and all beautiful things had been mirrored had dried up, leaving only a stagnant puddle that mirrored nothing. (*Poet and Dancer*, p. 190)

The nervous breakdown, emotional suffocation and boredom has made the behaviour of these two otherwise talented and ambitious girls—poet and dancer—eccentric and deadly offensive. Hugo is also hurt by Lara and the blood oozing out of his face is a symbolic punishment to a father who has neglected his daughter and thus made her an insane sexual crank. Similarly, Helena has also neglected Angel for selfish purposes and when towards the close of the novel she wants to revive her affectionate love for her daughter it is too late because now Angel knows no other commitment except one made to Lara. It is ironical that now Helena is desperate to love Angel but finds her daughter unmoved and if tears drop from Angel's eyes it is only for the sake of her cousin Lara who has always been intimate to her.

Thus, *Poet and Dancer* investigates the malaise of women protagonists in an uprooted, arid and disintegrated emigre community of modern America where the holy institutions of 'family' and 'marriage' have decayed and life has lost its true essence. Due to the selfishness and sexual permissiveness in parents their children are unfortunate creatures doomed to face the dilemma of emotional vacuum and self-destructive involvements leading to a malaise of self-hatred as painful as death-in-life. Jhabvala hints here that grandparents have comparatively closer relations with new generation than the parents but it is deplorable that old generation has lost its controlling hold on the households.

The next and the last full-fledged novel of Ruth Jhabvala is *Shards of Memory* (1995) and it is again framed on well-defined thematic lines of her fiction. The disintegration of feminine sensibilities in modern world has already taken its complete turn in *Three Continents* but Jhabvala reiterates its cosmopolitan dimension in this novel quite artistically. With an extensive use of cinematic flashback technique, the novelist has beautifully woven a complex texture picturising the masquerades of four generations all suffering from a malaise of emotional aridity, ethical wasteland and spiritual death searching for revival at the hands of some more powerful spiritual mentor.

Elsa Koef is a wealthy American who has married an Indian poet, the Parsi Hormusji Bilimoria called Kavi but she finds no anchoring power in her married life. With a desire to come out of this abyss of boredom and self-hatred she discards her family bonds and moves from New York to Hampstead to dedicate herself to the dissemination of a mysteriously enchanting Master's message. The recruitment in this dubious commune headed by a charismatic spiritual healer is indirectly their submission to the fascist power of male chauvinism. Baby is Elsa's daughter by Kavi, and by now she is also in her old age. She explains how Elsa neglected her by not giving her due affection and thus damaged her sensibility at the tender age. This dissolution of marital and filial ties was the beginning of a disease which went deep in further coming generations when the institutions of 'family' and 'marriage' became fully irrelevant and ineffective. Baby expresses their dilemma of inner fragmentation in these words:

> I suppose I could be considered a sort of pioneer for the following generations when it became very common to have two sets of couples as parents; although I think it would still be uncommon to have the father and grandmother as one couple and another the mother and her woman friend.[6]

The lesbian bond between Elsa and Cynthia gives little satisfaction and probably its insufficiency leads them to enter in the charismatic halo of the guru's masculinity. In the next generation Baby's misadventurous marriage with Greame also proves a failure and taking the advantage of this bickering the Master makes his hold on her. She herself narrates her estrangement with her husband as follows:

> We were never divorced and he never remarried...but he was reported to have had many different affairs in many different countries. He wouldn't have been able to live without women. (*Shards of Memory*, p. 37)

Baby has a daughter Renata by Greame and it is through him that the Anglo-Saxon strain was added to the stock of Kopfkeller and Billimoria family. Lourie Sucher's observation with regard to these gurus as charlatan and their beloveds as heels is worth quoting:

> The women—or men—who fall in love with these icons of power hope to be known and loved: they are not, for they have gravitated to men who know them only in the sense of knowing how to use them.[7]

It's all strange that Baby is giving her account of personal life to none else but to her own grandson Henry—the son of Renata by Carl.

The novel is divided in two parts—the first with a title 'Antecedents' in Henry's own family and the second with 'Legacy' received by him. We also know that Baby did not explain anything further may be she regarded her wedding a summit from which she did not want to come down. Anyway, henceforth the narrative is mostly based on Henry's research and it starts with the birth of his mother Renata. This is Jhabvala's multifaceted exposure technique dealing with four generations simultaneously and Henry investigates this record between him and Baby to ascertain his own legacy which reflects on the symptomatic descendence of the Master. The persistent domain of the Oriental spiritual guru cult is again present in the mysterious Master's possession on these self-seeking women. The dubious inference to his background and the extraordinary semblance of Henry, not to his natural father but to the dubious Master is a unique transformation of the Oriental spiritualism into an identity of racial admixture.

Henry's research into antecedents makes us aware of the fragmentation and diffusion of family bonds in the descending generations of the western society. Baby's own separation from her husband puts her at large freedom to devote herself to her personal friends, to the circle of her own choice and needs. Renata was accidentally conceived in the course of her parents separation and was born in New York and had spent her early childhood with her grandfather Kavi and her great grandmother Darothy Kopf. Kavi was in his element looking after his daughter Baby, his granddaughter Renata and his mother-in-law with her attendant. Renata was also made to realise the traumatic extravagance of sexuality of her mother Baby when she was taken to people—especially the uncles who loved her mother and also they used to stay the whole nights with Baby in bedroom.

After these gruesome jolts to her sensibility at the tender age of childhood, Renata is taken to England under the supervision of her grandmother Elsa only to become a new disciple of the mysterious godfather. It is paradoxical that without making any progress in developing her individuality Renata involves in sexuality with a German vagrant dweller Carl in London. On entering into intimacy with this pale-eyed and feeble man Renata loses her interest in the activities of commune.

Renata, fully prepared to spend herself on Carl's ideas and their mutual idealism, also becomes a stimulating key to their physical indulgence. Their discussion on the idea of a world-wide campaign for reforms and re-orientation of educational system overflows into their sex act which is incidental to them, almost perfunctory. Ironically, Renata provides, food, shelter and sexual proximity to this feeble man who, after all, is selling a rival programme to that of the Master's movement. The matter comes in open when she becomes pregnant and suffers from a sort of psychological disorder. As the Master also functions as a psychiatrist or some kind of spiritual guide to women Renata is immediately fitted into his schedule of appointment inside his bedroom. Looking up at her with his searching eyes and enveloping her in his infinitely loving smile, the Master encourages Renata to gaze into his pewter-coloured and tarter eyes—they are pewter-coloured and seem to hold reflections of a hypnotizing spell. In one of Henry's possessions of the memoirs he finds how Renata opens her heart to the Master who treats her in this way:

> But now that she was actually with him she did not believe any of it; no, not even when he raised his hand from her thigh and laid it on her breast, next he was holding both her breasts, not fondling them but more like a doctor, examining them, and then more and more like a doctor he raised the lids of his eyes. "Give me your hand," he said; she did so and let him feel her pulse with expert fingers.... But she felt sure that he had diagnosed

> her secret; that is her dedication to Carl's cause; and in a way he said, "you are pregnant". (*Shards of Memory*, pp. 60-61)

Greame has no position in the hegemony of the Master and his doomed followers and so he communicates the news of Renata's dubious pregnancy to Baby in New York and calls her immediately to London. Renata, though agrees to return to New York with Baby, yet she has no sense of guilt because she is well aware that Baby's own life has been full with so many lovers. It is only her awareness to safeguard her grandchild from incompetent parents that she takes Renata with her.

The most astonishing and perplexing thing in *Shards of Memory* is the event to go back to an occurrence at the time of Henry's birth. The birth of this child coincides with the death of the Master on the same day and at the same time. On the day of his death the Master expresses his sadness as none of his women disciples could manage to hatch a soul. Addressing his women followers especially Elsa and Cynthia he says on his death bed:

> And now what's going to happen to you? What will become of you? Who will take care of you now, who will carry you in his arms, feed you with whatever pitiful pap you're able to digest? Is there anyone willing to pick up the burden that I'm at last getting off my back? Has he come yet? Is he born? (*Shards of Memory*, p. 86)

It is equally remarkable that Henry looks not in the least like his pale, abstracted father Carl but like this mysterious Master. His eyes like those of the Master are partly hooded, partly slanted and beyond all reasonings. Elsa and Cynthia have no other topic to wonder during their midnight sessions except trying to ascertain whether there is the rebirth of their spiritual taskmaster in Henry. "Has he come yet?" Cynthia quoted and Elsa capped it with "Is he born?" Yes, they were sure: he had come; he was born" (*Shards of Memory*, p. 103). Moreover, the Master's declaration of Henry as his rightful successor confirms their belief and they decide to hand over the cherished burden of the Master's legacy to this boy with same appearance. But an unfortunate accident occurs in which Elsa and Cynthia die and Henry is crippled.

The second part of the novel is purposely entitled 'Legacy' which is actually left by Elsa, Cynthia, his ancestors and the Master in the name of Henry. To this effect Henry receives an important envelope from their solicitor which he reads but could not divulge its contents to anyone. Jhabvala narrates Henry's dismay about his own illegitimacy as:

> For there was one line that gave him pause, one word rather and that was where they referred to Henry not only as the successor of the Master but as his son and successor. No doubt they meant it in a spiritual sense but for Henry it was a reminder of his own strange and hitherto unexplained appearance. (*Shards of Memory*, p. 114)

Now Henry gets desperate to solve this enigma of his own parentage and he directly asks Renata whether she had slept with the Master. Renata confesses that the Master had taken her pulse, had gazed into her eyes. Henry is irritated and thinks that the sexual act might have taken place while she was too abstracted and hypnotized to notice it. Renata defends herself by telling him that the whole procedure of treatment by the Master was weird and he had strange powers. Being unable to understand his own blood lineage Henry thinks it pertinent to ask Greame. To his surprise, Greame tells him that Baby had certainty slept with the Master and it was not possible to find any heir through grandmother. Henry gets more perturbed to know it and is anxious to confirm his legacy and so persistently attempts to diffuse Renata. On her reiteration that she has not even married Carl he gets furious and frustrated on his own status as a bastard. He asks her why she had not got a wedding certificate at least for her son's social acceptance. Renata speaks in an agony of meaninglessness of the family bonds: "And marriages never do work out in our family—look at Kavi and Elsa and Baby and Greame—What disasters!" (*Shards of Memory*, p. 170)

In another conversation Renata shyly explains to him something more about the Master: whether he is his father or not:

> "What do I know?" and as he stared at her more—"I don't know," she said candidly—in the present tense, for it was clear that she was no more knowing now than she had been then. After a while she continued: "Anyway, he goes so far back with us that he might as well be family. Right back to Elsa; and of course to Kavi who met him in India". (*Shards of Memory*, p. 223)

Henry is astonished at this revelation about the heritage of the Master. More than all this Greame gives him more information about the Master. He had informed Greame all sort of things; for instance, in his youth he had been a spy for the Russians in and around Afghanistan. He was born in Tabriz in the house of a carpet-seller and his original name was Nasir Salah. But Henry could not get final truth about the Master since it was just one version of the autobiographical accounts of him and there were several others, too. Thus, the Master's early years, his ancestry, his education and his name remained an enigmatic obscurity and so he is unable to ascertain his own heritage.

However, it is authentic that the Master had been a great womanizer and had come in contact with Mme. Richter who had been suffering from nervous breakdown due to her childless marriage. During the revolution when the Richter family had to flee the country, he had helped them to pass to Tiflis, Constantinople, Berlin and then to Paris. This male chauvinist had led them like a ring-master and from that time onward he had taken some aspects of a possessive male power on women and men with feminine temperament. The same youngman was also introduced to Sofia in Bombay as the cousin alias the Master; to Kavi and some others as a revolutionary but his ideology was poles apart from the Gandhian movement. When one of his followers mentioned their proposed joining the Gandhian movement, the cousin made the dismissive gesture:

> That was not the way, he said; sheep to be led by a sheep. A wolf that was what he needed, and not one but many many wolves—yes, all of them, he said, gazing

> around their circle with hypnotic eyes. (*Shards of Memory*, p. 231)

This revolutionary cousin was in reality a wolf for women and soon was heard to disappear overnight only to re-appear after converting himself into the Master of a commune propagating to develop spiritual potentials of his followers. The Master is still mysterious and illusive as his arrival and disappearance at his commune centres is kept secret. There is always a want for women in his dominion and he is a womanizer and manipulator like the devilish Swamiji of *A New Dominion*. In this novel, the women from the western society are trapped and enthralled by this fascist male disguised as spiritual mentor and he reduces them into his possessions only.

Henry is perturbed on these tantalizing facts of his legacy which is still as ambiguous as always. In spite of the legal legacy to become the spiritual, if not the physical, successor of the Master, Henry has lost all his desire to become another master. God forbid even if he could since the destruction of his familial tradition and inheritance was undoubtedly sealed by women only after their entrance into the spell of this sinister Oriental guru. It is noteworthy that women are the most vulnerable, most submissive and, above all, the most confessional in their sexuality with no inhibitions on them. This novel is an extensive saga of the sexual misadventures of the crazy women living and experiencing a malaise of death in life and a loss of human need to believe. In this rootless community of the German emigre the pious socio-cultural bonds—marriage, family and parents—have gone futile. Therefore, their self-illusion and submission to some spiritual authority leads these women to hazardous and self-destructive consequences with no more possibility to restore their old values and traditions. It is ironical that grandmothers and grandfathers are comparatively closer to their grandchildren than the selfish, indulgent and estranged mothers and fathers whose sexuality is a greater binding force for them than their posterity and blood ties.

To say *Shards of Memory* is in full exposure of Jhabvala's well-defined theme of the feminine sensibilities which she did initiate with a mild treatment of the womanly passions and their exposure in her first novel *To Whom She Will*. The fascist male dominance and the idiosyncratic submission of female is a persistent phenomenon whether we probe into the confined and suffocating sensibilities of women in the tabooed Indian society or we scan the alienated and fragmented individuality of woman in the western society. The predicament of woman's exploitation is never absent though it has changed in its characteristics.

Although the artistic vision oscillates between romance and ironical reality, the imperative to shed inhibitions has become particularly a feminine quest since the women and homosexual men are the most willing victims to the male inclination for self-aggrandizement. The later novels of Jhabvala present a more mature vision of the romantic involvements of the illusionary women and homosexuals with femininity in their existence who are in a dilemma of obsession for male possessiveness and self destructive sexuality. The strong, mysterious and charismatic males, unlike those whom they hold in thrall, are revealed to be motivated by expediency, acquisitiveness, class revenge or simply the narcissistic pleasure of collecting female admirers. In this final phase Ruth Jhabvala has encompassed the psychological analysis of women in the cross-cultural labyrinth of human relationships.[8]

Ruth Jhabvala's novels of the American phase constitute an exploration, told from a woman's point of view, of the sexual politics in the American emigre community which has already undergone a holocaust. These novels articulate that women are sick of alienation, infidelity, self-hatred, internal fragmentation and disintegration of their sensibilities. The anchoring institutions of marriage and family have lost their purpose and essence in the cosmopolitan community of modern America having people of mixed race, mixed identity and mixed sexuality. Undoubtedly, the women, in spite of all their freedom and empowerment, are still the greatest losers and sufferers because they are naive, self-delusive and self-destructive victims of acquisitive masculinity. It confirms and illustrates the premise of feminism, the societal degradation and sexual inferiority of women at large. It also confirms the feminist's imperative: that woman resists the social and psychological derogation and in her struggle she does not have, by and large, the support, love or friendship of other women. In Jhabvala's novels the female protagonist is emotionally isolated and victimized and in her quest for self-actualisation, she is unable and sometimes unwilling to draw strength from others like herself. If there are relations between women, they are selfish, manipulative and exploitative.

Neither of the groups, family or America, is homogenous any longer, if it ever was and perhaps, the unbridled freedom and nefarious involvements of women have resulted in emotional aridity, sexual sickness, incestuous obscenity and meaninglessness of life. The family is no more a cementing force and the mother-daughter bond is conspicuously weak—daughters, usually seen from the mother's viewpoint, are selfishly obsessed with their men. When mothers are seen from the daughter's point of view, they are usually absent—again away with their fascist lovers. Grandmothers and granddaughters generally have a closer relationship than mothers and daughters but grandmothers are powerless to protect young women from male predation. Moreover, in these fictions a gulf—wider than ever—yawns between men and women and the few heterosexual men in these works are excessively attractive to women but their interests run exclusively in business, materialistic gains and sexual pleasures only, e.g. Leo of *In Search of Love and Beauty* and bisexual Crishi in *Three Continents* are exclusive womanizers disguised in pseudo-spiritualism.

One more truth is quite clear that the women are unable to nurture and validate relationships even with homosexual males. The influence of male chauvinism on female sensibilities is also portrayed in the triangle of homosexual men in contrast to their heterosexual women lovers or relations. Though male homosexuals are not new to Jhabvala's novels as there is Harry in *Heat and Dust* and Raymond in *A New Dominion*, yet her American novels probe comparatively deeper into the effects of homosexuality on feminine sensibilities as well as female individuality. The women who are close to this as mother, sister, grandmother or even beloved react in vague and desperate ways. Psychologically, a woman in such triangles suffers from a complex of self-insufficiency since she finds herself not good in her capacity to hold on the concerned male. These homosexuals may disperse a kind of love or friendship to some women but it is at a heavy financial cost and they place woman as a secondary being to their male counterpart—thus a new disadvantage to womanhood as it places woman at a new kind of distance from man. The focus on male homosexuality is an interest towards a movement whereas lesbianism is derided, ignored or viewed as a vain attempt to revolt in this labyrinth of sexual politics in human relations in Jhabvala's novels of the American phase. However, no relation—familial or sexual—is able to regain the emotional warmth, internal peace and spiritual rejuvenation for these inhabitants of modern America.

NOTES

1. Ruth Prawer Jhabvala, *In Search of Love and Beauty* (Middlesex; England: Penguin Books Ltd., 1986), p. 1.
2. Ronald Shepherd, *op. cit.*, p. 138.
3. Lourie Sucher, *op. cit.*, p. 146.
4. *cf.* Ronald Shepherd, "In Crishi and the movement there exists for Harriet and Michael Wishwell the promise of some magnificent renewal. The associated dangers of their liaison only stimulate in the twins a reckless desire to go the whole hog", *op. cit.*, p. 152.
5. Ruth Prawer Jhabvala, *Poet and Dancer* (London: Penguin Books, 1994), pp. 25-26.
6. Ruth Prawer Jhabvala, *Shards of Memory* (London: Penguin Books, 1996), p. 27.
7. Lourie Sucher, *The Fiction of Ruth Prawer Jhabvala: The Politics of Passion* (London: The Macmillan Press Ltd., 1989), p. 11.
8. *cf.* Lourie Sucher: "Ruth Jhabvala's later fiction examines relationships between heterosexual women and homosexual men; they are rich with insights into women's psychology and women's lives, although they do betray some uneasiness in their portrayal of homosexuality, which the novels seem to suggest is all right for men, but not for women", *The Fiction of Ruth Prawer Jhabvala: The Politics of Passion* (London: The Macmillan Press Ltd., 1989), p. 9.

6

Summing-Up

The foregoing chapters assess the making up of Ruth Prawer Jhabvala as a writer with peculiar literary sensibility and also present an analytical study of the thematic concept of the predicament of feminine sensibilities manifested in her novels at the different stages of her career. Obviously, Jhabvala explicates the issues that the feminists have been engrossed with but her literary vision and perception of the complex feminine phenomenon during her passage through three main continents of this planet have earned a conspicuous position for her among the women fictionists of the present age. The articulation of the whole gamut of the feminine feelings and passions, hopes and aspirations, frustrations and agonies along with the female quest for self-actualisation and individual identity is quintessentially Jhabvala's own distinct voice. No doubt, the enrichment of this woman writer's literary sensibility through a wider exposure along with her peculiar experiences, have given a triangular mode to her artistic vision and thematic perspectives.

This study of Jhabvala's novels makes clear that her literary endeavour began with an ironic portrayal of womenfolk in the traditional conservative and patriarchal society of India; then she focused on the predicament of the enigmatic romance and unscrupulous submission of the European women who happen to come to this obsessively enchanting sub-continent—a phenomenon much closer to the exiled author's own heart; and lastly on her move to New York, she scans the soul and psyche of the American women who are suffering from the agony of boredom, psychic disintegration, abnormal sexuality and self-hatred. With these progressive thematic dimensions Jhabvala's craftsmanship has also got enrichment and maturity which makes her stand apart in the gallery of women fictionists of modern times. The study analyses the predicament of feminine sensibilities from a woman's point of view in the novels of this writer who has dealt with womanhood and feminine quest for self-actualisation in various settings encompassing three prominent continents.

The first chapter presents a logical study of the process of the making of this novelist. It has been observed that in the making of the personality of this novelist a number of kaleidoscopic changes of the milieu have played decisive roles. The self-proclaimed Europeanness of Ruth Prawer Jhabvala has been moulded and enraged by her fortuitous exile and family life in urban India and then by her 'self-exiled' move to America for a greater exposure and artistic excellence there. Due to this unusual biography and its far-reaching influences on her personality and literary sensibility the question of her national identity has really become a puzzling problem. Her passage from Europe to India and from here to America has not only baffled the historians and critics of English literature but the novelist herself is also unable to make a final announcement about her own identity and status at last.

However, a rigorous study of her fictional and non-fictional works has made it quite clear that this expatriate woman of European consciousness felt the Indian milieu on her pulse through her personal experiences here. Being a daughter-in-law of India she was at an advantageous position of being in India and out of India and to her observation of urban India life she brings both a European's irony that can come only with a certain detachment and an insider's knowledge of details and nuances that few non-Indians could claim to command. Obviously, her passage to India has been drastically different from that of Kipling or E.M. Forster. Her Indian fiction is spun by an initiated outsider with an unusual insight and this perspective in Indian context could not be available to any other great Anglo-Indian writers who have addressed themselves to the cross-cultural issues.

In spite of all these advantageous claims for Jhabvala, it will be unwise to call her a genuine Indian novelist since her authorial voice is in the mainstream of the European writers. Truly speaking, she remained in the status of a European transplanted in the urban middle-class society of India for a substantial period of twenty-five years but could not get rooted here. So her eyes could not look beneath the surface as the inward realities of the Indian life are not touched by her and her range of knowledge remained confined only to the predicament of pseudo-modern women in middle-class section of Delhi and to the experiences of expatriate women in the same background. One more fact should also be considered here that the family into which Ruth Prawer married is Parsi and that the Persians themselves are of an outsider group in India. Very much like the Jews in their diaspora the Parsis value education, pursue their professional status and equally maintain their distinct and separate identity as a community. Perhaps, this aloofness from common Indians is also a cause of Jhabvala's limited range of feminine world in Indian context.

The second chapter comprises the comprehensive defining deliberation on the thematic concept of the feminine sensibility. Chapters III, IV and V critically analyse the novels written by Jhabvala so far and therefore constitute the core part of this study. The first phase of the literary career of Jhabvala spreads over her first five novels in which she has portrayed the oddities, eccentricities of the middle-class society of India and its traditional verdict for confinement, suppression and subservience of woman and fascist dominance of man. It has been traced that these novels expose the tyranny of the age-old patriarchal hegemony and the subservient and slavish position of woman in Indian social system. The atmosphere is sunny in the early novels where protagonists are young, educated and modern women who aspire for their emancipation and self-realisation as individual human beings. With the exception of *Esmond in India* there is no involvement of any westerner in these novels which picturise the conflict between the traditional social decorum and the romantic quest of young protagonists for their individual identity and freedom of choice. It has been found that the attempts of women protagonists to re-define the role and identity of woman are labelled as rebellion against the established code of behaviour and the hard-handed control of males on females. With an ironic vision of a social realist Jhabvala lashes at the selfishness, hypocrisy and insincerity of males through the romantic extravagance of the naive lovers who surrender to the very first pressures of their families. Though Amrita and Nimmi eventually accept the decisions of their families to marry the man of their selection, they shine far above their lovers—Hari and Pheroze—due to their courage and resistance against social pressures. It is quite clear that daughter is still treated as a personal possession of parents especially of father and there is no scope for any individual identity of her. In spite of the high romantic idealism of the love of the protagonists, the authoritative male force crushes every possibility of self-realisation and freedom of choice in selecting a husband. Fascistic males of the household thwart the attempts of the modern educated protagonists to re-define their identity and achieve freedom. Other women of the house are instrumental in this suppression and so are indirectly spokespersons of the rigid patriarchal dominance in Indian society even in post-independence era.

Jhabvala extracts much comedy from the romantic excesses and insufficient defiance of these immature lovers who rate their love very high but readily renounce it on the very first pressure of society. In this comic exposition, it is ironical that in renouncing their love the young men are more prompt and selfish than the defiant girls. In the defiance and feminine upsurge of the protagonists of the early two novels Jhabvala seems to suggest that the stirrings for freedom from the bondage is getting momentum inside the Indian womenfolk along with the process of the refinement of their sense and sensibilities. Here Jhabvala's irony is double-edged authorial instrument to expose the predicament of women in the patriarchal social set up as well as the pseudo-modernism of young protagonists who love just to satiate their curiosity and do not strike hard when it is snatched from them.

The protagonist of *Esmond in India* goes a step ahead of her predecessors as this modern butterfly finds an exciting love and happiness in being daring enough to have an affair with a European who has already married an Indian girl after a short romance with her. Shakuntala searches for her self-actualisation in an idea of daring marriage with Esmond after his divorce. The mutual repulsion and bickering in the wedlock of Esmond and Gulab become a hope for this protagonist who makes a triangle by her involvement with her lover. Esmond, like other male characters in Jhabvala's novels, is not sincere in his commitments to his beloved who is seduced by this womaniser just for a relief from his obtuse wife.

It is quite humorous and ironical that in spite of all modernity of Shakuntala's parents she is still not free from the over-possessive cocoon of fatherhood and her marriage is arranged with a man chosen by her parents. It is again proved that woman is still shunned as an inferior and subservient sex in this society.

The stoic subjugation of woman to the incompetent but highly authoritarian husband is the primary issue highlighted in the novel *The Householder*. Here the novelist presents the predicament of an Indian woman in a household where the husband has failed on all fronts of life but his ego is so high that he resorts to his father-brand authoritarianism over his wife. The childish behaviour of this husband and over-possessive intrusion of his mother leads to bickering in the household and separation of the couple. But Indu is an Indian woman having no option except returning to her husband who is unable to prove his manliness and, therefore, suffers from an inferiority complex. *Get Ready for Battle* is the last novel of Indian phase and it symbolises the feminine call to womenfolk of India for readiness to fight their battle for their full emancipation from the time honoured patriarchal dominance over them. With the change of time the Indian women have taken many defiant and progressive steps as the novelist has portrayed three bold women—Sarla, Kusum and Mala—

fighting their own battles for self-actualisation and identity as individuals in their own ways. With the progress of time the women portrayed in *Get Ready for Battle* have got a symptomatic change and now they are not content with their traditional role of obedience to husband or household chores. Now divorce, re-marriage, separation and movement in social circles have become the well-accepted realities of society but women are still not emancipated from the bondage and dependence on their men. The novelist is a social realist in presenting the insufficiency of the feminine fights for freedom and women's efforts are ironically thwarted by their male counterparts. No doubt, the intensity of the feminine defiance and upsurge is getting stronger in novel after novel but woman is still in a miserable predicament of victimization at the hands of male and her voice for individual identity is suppressed quite boldly.

The fourth chapter covers three novels of the second literary phase of Ruth Prawer Jhabvala and here she articulates the predicament of the sensibilities of the western women in Indian background. In it an analysis has been made of the responses and reactions of the expatriate European women who come to India as lovers, wives, travellers and seekers of the spiritual enlightenment. In dealing with these protagonists of the European origin in interaction with India and Indians this novelist has given a subtle and ironical twist to the hackneyed and everlastingly interesting theme of East-West malaise and its traumatic effects on the sensibilities of the western women.

In *A Backward Place* the trio of the European protagonists—Judy, Etta and Clarissa—represents in varying degrees their romantic idealism and the metamorphic impact of this monstrously obsessive subcontinent of primitive socio-cultural heritage. The study makes it clear that these protagonists are various versions of the feminine sensibilities of Europe at their different stages of romantic idealism and weird self-destructive process of Indianisation. The novel also exposes the chauvinistic glorification of marriage as a permanent fusion of two souls and the place of husband as

God in the life of a woman. Here the authoritarian attitude of Indian husbands and its adverse effects on the sensibilities of western women, the falsity and hypocrisy of the primitive code of morality have all been vehemently attacked with the ironic vision of a European rationalist.

The predicament of the western spiritual seekers in this land of old renowned spiritualism is most pathetically portrayed in *A New Dominion* where three expatriate girls are on their spiritual adventure to lose themselves in order to find their selves. It is quite ironical that religiosity has now deteriorated and sexual rapacity is the only religion that these naive girls are rewarded by the hypocrite Swamiji who brutally exploits them. The traumatic undoing of Lee, Margaret and Evie exposes the moral degradation, brutality and corruption prevalent in the so-called religious centres and spiritual god-men of India. This submission of the expatriate women to the male rapacity of the Indians disguised as spiritual healers has again falsified the feminine cause of self-realisation, spiritual rejuvenation and integrated identity as a being. *Heat and Dust* is again a sordid tale of misadventures of the European women, who, after coming under the metamorphic effects of India become the victims of tragic obsessions. The two heroines—Olivia, a romantic idealist in imperial India and the Narrator an anti-romantic modern observer—portray the drama of East-West malaise with a gap of half a century. The feelings of personal entrapment, fear of growing old and frustration of being a loser in the game of passions draws Olivia into a sexual liaison with the crude, sensual and insensitive Nawab and she sacrifices her all for love. There is a double irony in this novel for the rational and cautious Narrator, on a mission to solve the enigma of Olivia's scandalous destruction, herself becomes a victim of almost same scandal and finally moves towards hills to seek remedy in isolation. The most strange and intractable mystery of the feminine sensibility becomes not what happened to self-deluded Olivia, but rather how to account for this sensible modern rational woman's wily submission to illusionary Indian demands which, as she already knows, are fatal in consequences. The inevitable fall of these European women to the sinister masculinity of Indians, in spite of all the warnings of Christianity and rationalism, may be ascribed to the mutual erotic calls of flesh and arousal of the sexual hunger in this tropical land. However, the feminine quest for self-actualisation has again ended in self-pity and self-immolation in this land of rapacious masculinity.

Jhabvala's career entered in its cosmopolitan phase with her move to the third prominent continent and this shifting has also finally literalised her outsiderhood and ever-exiled status as a writer. In this new western set up she portrays the multicultural saga of human relationships in an international labyrinth of variously displaced and misplaced people—most of them of mixed race, mixed culture and mixed sexuality. Now, through her fiction as well as screenplays, Jhabvala articulates the phenomena of multi-racial confluence with a wide and enriched vision and on a vast canvas. The novelist has also reached a considerable maturity as in this phase she scans the deep recesses of the soul and psyche of women protagonists mostly belonging to the emigre community of America. The unbridled freedom of life, indisciplined exercise of passions and unqualified and undefinable sexual involvements have made the women sick of abundance and emotional vacuum leading towards abnormal psychic manifestations. Moreover, due to the collapse of socio-cultural institutions like 'home', 'marriage' and 'family' these protagonists are in a hellish predicament of morbid anxiety, loss of faith and agony of death-in-life.

The women protagonists of these four novels suffer from obsessive and paradoxical compulsions of love, unscrupulous infatuations and abnormal sexual hunger since the unbridled freedom has lost their control on their passions. With the help of screenplay-like flashback technique the novelist plunges the reader into the crucial moments of three or even four generations of the emigre community. The whole gallery of the American protagonists and other women characters—Lousie, Marietta, Harriet, Angel, Lara, Elsa, Baby, Renata and others—portrays their life of economic abundance and luxury.

But it is ironical that almost all of them are in their hellish predicament of boredom, ennui, emotional aridity, alienation and abnormal sexuality which has caused disastrous psychological disorders to their sensibilities. To get rid of these throes of death-in-life, these miserable women hand over themselves to those males who possess extra-ordinarily charismatic personalities and propagate to bring spiritual succor to women. These mysteriously enchanting males with self-avowed religiosity are motivated by expediency, acquisitiveness, class-revenge or simply the narcissistic pleasure of collecting female admirers. The illusionary women and homosexual men having femininity in their temperament are victimised by the fascistic male absolutism and they are reduced to the dilemma of self-destructive sexuality which leads them nowhere. The unbridled freedom has led the life of these protagonists out of gear and their nefarious involvements and maniac sexuality have caused havoc to their sensibilities. It again confirms and illustrates the premise of feminism, the societal degradation and inferiority of the fair sex even in this world of all equality. It is noted that at this stage Jhabvala probes into the subconscious and unconscious of the feminine sensibilities and projects their inner recesses from a woman's point of view. To be true, these protagonists are inflicted with undefinable disease of internal fragmentation, abnormal sexuality, self-hatred and an incestuous urge to be possessed by some strong male power. So they are exploited sexually and economically by pseudo-religious gurus through their charismatic mechanism to satiate their rapacity.

Taken as a whole this study has reached certain comprehensive and acknowledgeable conclusions regarding the portrayal of feminine sensibilities and feminine quest for self-actualisation and independent identity in the novels of Ruth Prawer Jhabvala. A rigorous survey of her fiction makes it clear that the exploitation of the womenfolk has always been the persistent motif of male powers though their mechanism has changed as per the need and convenience of the hour. The male dominance and an idiosyncratic submission of female is an all-pervading phenomenon in Jhabvala's fictions whether they deal with the feminine sensibilities in the confined and tabooed society of India or probe deep into the psychic complexities of the women of the self-reliant and all-free society of the west. The thematic exposition of the predicament of feminine life was initiated by the novelist with the portrayal of mild upsurge and inadequate defiance of Amrita in her first novel dealing with conservative households of India. It has been noted that in India of pre- and post-independence era woman is treated as a personal possession of man as father or as husband and her quest for identity as well as her search for love and beauty have been strongly crushed by the male power. In picturising the miserable predicament of Indian women Jhabvala intends to expose the hypocrisy and male chauvinism of the post-independent India where woman is still in bondage and subservience of man who cunningly propagates himself to be humane.

The novelist has got success in a satirical articulation of the feminine challenge to male dominance and though the protagonists have failed in giving a shattering jolt to the age-old male chauvinism, yet they have succeeded in creating ripples of freedom in the bounded and subjugated life of Indian women. These early novels clarify that the patriarchal hegemony and old taboos have started eroding but sadly no new feminine ideology for an independent and self-actualising identity of woman has taken shape even in the era of post-independent India. In this world of fast changes and shifting values the women protagonists are at various stages of their refinement and self-realisation process which is getting momentum in every successive novel and has yet to go a long way for true emancipation of womenfolk in India. It is an equally noted feature in these novels that the awareness for self-identity and self-reliance has reached only the middle-class households and the average Indian women are still in a slumber of slavery and predicament of unaccountable submission to male dominance. It is also quite evident that the young protagonists are in a miserable condition of helplessness, alienation and self-pity because their own community of women is most vindictive in attitude as well as instrumental in executing the wishes of the males on females of their families. Jhabvala's vision is realistic and her tone sarcastic in exposing the pseudo-satisfaction gained by the old generations of women by crushing the quests of their youngsters and thus feeling a pride to be head of the household affairs.

For all their exotic settings Jhabvala's novels of the middle-class Indian life present an incongruous but inescapable similarity to those of Jane Austen since in many ways—the large families, the strict code of behaviour, the husband-hunting, the constant presence of relations—the setting has more in common with the eighteenth century England than it has with the modern west. However, it is a matter of serious concern for the Indian feminists that unlike the heroines of Jane Austen, the protagonists of Jhabvala's novels do not grow in virtues and even at the end of the novels they are less refined, spoiled, self-centred and insensible. They do not get any refinement of sensibilities and succumb to the social and economic realities of the life and thus do not hesitate in accepting a husband of their parents choice. In this way these modern women are pseudo-idealists and the true modernity with a re-definition of feminine roles and rules is still a far cry for Indian womenfolk at large.

The phenomena of the western women engaged in a weird and complicated criss-crossing to the enigmatic India and seductive Indians present more or less the unsatisfactory solutions to their romantic illusions and dangerous quests to become Indian without having to surrender their own Europeanness. The tragedy in the novels of the middle phase rises from the intimate interactions of the expatriate women with the Indians in post-independence era since there is no more any shielding protection of the colonial officialdom of British imperialism. The maltreatment to Judy, the brutal rape of Lee, the seduction of Olivia and her step-granddaughter are some symbolic portrayals of the disparity between the romantic illusions of the western women about India and Indians who, in turn, could provide them nothing but sexuality, betrayal and falsehood. In portraying the subjugation of the European women by Indian lovers, husbands or the spiritual gurus, Jhabvala hints at the moral and spiritual degradation in modern India. The search of the expatriate women for love, beauty or spirituality ends in their victimisation at the hands of male rapacity and they are in a predicament of self-destructive commitments or flight for survival.

It is observed that even the spiritual heritage of India has lost its glory in Jhabvala's world of fictional India because the spiritual and aesthetic seekers also face traumatic experiences. No doubt, since antiquity the Indian spiritualism has been shining far above the philosophic deliberations of the world; however, Jhabvala lashes at the fraudulent guru-cults of modern growth where, in maximum cases, spirituality is only a mechanism for the gratification of sexual and materialistic hunger of man.

The victimisation of the naive expatriate women in India suggests that morality and religious degradation has touched its lowest ebb in modern times. But one of the most puzzling facts in the sensibilities and behaviour of these protagonists is that their obsession with their male exploiters reaches at a point of no return and they sacrifice their all for love. They are doomed for miserable predicament of internal fragmentation sometimes leading to death. It is more than clear that the characters like Swamiji and Nawab have no qualms either moral or religious in abusing the credulous expatriate women but what makes these women drag themselves again to these violators is a mystery that Jhabvala has left unexplained. It has been researched that all the warnings of Christianity and European rationalism fail to rescue these otherwise rational women from falling again and again in the clutches of their demon-lovers who betray them in every way.

The presentation of these degraded rogues in almost a general negative context of Indian religiosity is not a justice but a prejudiced notion since a few rogues cannot defile the spiritual holiness of Indian heritage. Some hypocritical, selfish and rapacious rogues disguised as religious mentors, have brought ignominy to the spiritualism of our land abroad and the novelist seems to have noticed only this distortion as highlighted in her fiction. In this respect she has presented an uneasy combination of the sacred and the profane, the spiritual and the sexual, the pious and the pervert in these erotic intrigues of males who falsely propagate to take these women on their adventure of transcendental realisation. Being enthralled by the fascistic masculinity of these hypocrites the European women develop an incessant sexuality and thus are doomed to experience the hellish predicament of self-delusion and sometimes even death.

This research makes it clear that while the novels of the early phase of Jhabvala, like those of any genuine Indian writer, tend to deal with Indians as people first and only secondarily as Indians, in the novels of Indo-European saga this order is reversed as she sarcastically hints at the various points of clash and conflict amongst the characters coming from two uncompromising socio-cultural backgrounds. Though Jhabvala's locale is Delhi—the city of old traditional subcontinent in microcosm, with a rather more mature artistic vision she portrays the metamorphic impacts of India on the illusionary westerners especially the women. Moreover, like so many European writers dealing with cross-cultural issues, she has virtually reached her own conclusions regarding this interaction between eastern masculinity and western femininity in post-independence era. First, as the communication and fusion between India and the west is always imperfect, there is no harmonious meeting of the souls of the lovers or couples of these two distant lands; secondly, that the Indians, particularly males are somehow deficient in great qualities of character and performance as understood by the western women; and thirdly, as India is a source of disillusion, disgust and disintegration for the naive and romantic women of the west, their quest for love, beauty and spirituality is doomed to lead them into an enigmatic state of infatuation, obsession and self-immolation in this mysteriously metamorphic land.

Nevertheless, this predicament of the European women in India does not invalidate the romantic quest itself as the errant female protagonists learn by shedding naive illusions about man, romance, sex and religion. The experiences of the protagonists' yield neither cynicism not even renunciation but only a deeper curiosity about their purpose of existence which persists with much more dangerous morbidity in Jhabvala's novels written in United States after leaving India.

The phenomenon of the feminine sensibilities has reached its full exposition in Jhabvala's novels of the cosmopolitan phase where socio-cultural ethics and morality have lost their relevance and women flit from continent to continent with a confessional independence and individuality. But even in this world of absolute freedom of life women are in a predicament of wily submission to mysteriously alluring compulsions of flesh and it again leads to their exploitation at the hands of over-possessive males who have power to control these miserable women. Easy divorce, frequently changing partners, incestuous sexuality and loss of ethics have caused hazardous complexities which are most gruesome and disastrous in their repercussions.

The study clarifies that Jhabvala's novels from beginning to the last constitute an exploration of the feminine sensibilities and feminine quest for identity and self-actualisation as individual human beings free from any dependence syndrome. But in all the phases of her literary career it is observed that this quest for love, beauty, bliss and identity has been thwarted because woman is unable to come out of the shadow of man in spite of all equality in materialistic sense. The protagonists in all settings are portrayed as frail, wily, seductive and enigmatically submissive to masculine powers which lead them to self-hatred, inner fragmentation and even sometimes to death. The Indian women are sufferers of confinement and cruel suppression; the expatriate European women in India are victims of romantic passions or spiritual idealism leading to their dooms; and most strikingly, the modern women of west are possessed with mysterious urge to be controlled by some charismatic masculine power as they are suffering from emotional vacuum, abnormal sexuality, psychic disorder and loss of faith in life.

Even more than this almost all the protagonists of Jhabvala's novels have another trait in common: they are completely alienated from other women and in their pursuit of self-actualisation and identity they are miserably alone. Whether it is conservative India or America of all freedom of life there is no moral support, love or friendship of other fellow women to the protagonists. Contrary to this there is an antagonism or rivalry amidst the women and this increases the miseries of the woman concerned. The women of Indian society find a pleasure in thwarting the quest of the young protagonists and thus becoming instrumental in maintaining the dominance of male power on women. It is equally strange that the expatriate European protagonists in India are deprived of all support and friendship of the women of their nativity as soon as they violate the European code of behaviour and cross over to Indian socio-cultural heritage. Even the women of the modern western society are unable to nurture any valid relationships amongst them, perhaps, because of their rivalry for charismatic males.

Another quite distinct feature that one discovers in Jhabvala's final phase is the manifestation of homosexual men and heterosexual women and even vice versa that places woman at a new kind of distance by assigning an inferior status to her in the labyrinth of complex and undefinable relationships. Though the homosexuals are also present in the novels of Indo-European phase, yet in the final phase the disastrous and distorting effects of male power on feminine sensibilities are visualised in the triangles of homosexual men in contrast to the heterosexual women who are close to them in either capacity of mother, grandmother, sister or beloved.

The new emergence of gay-rights-activism in the crippled and disintegrated society of America is another great agony for women to make them feel inferior and inadequate for homosexual males treat women only for their rapacious purposes. One may logically acknowledge the female homosexuality as an option since there are lesbian entanglements of protagonists—Lousie-Regi, Elsa-Dorothy, Angel-Lara—but this is pathological and comic and not any satisfactory cementing substitute for masculinity. Moreover, an equation suggests here that the more passionate, wily, and moneyed the women, the more they have a chill of morbid sexuality in their character and any nexus between females is only a hidden enmity in their pursuit of being closer and intimate to their male violators.

Abnormal obsession and irresistible infatuations of protagonists towards their violators is another well-marked feature of the novels of Ruth Prawer Jhabvala. A long range of protagonists—Judy, Lee, Olivia, Lousie, Marietta, Harriet, Angel, Lara, Elsa and Renata—are sexually misused victims of the enigmatically enchanting womanisers but all find themselves in a vicious and mysterious dilemma of undefinable urge to be possessed by their charismatic males even at the cost of lives. Under the incessant obsession and erotic hunger for sex they readily sacrifice their all for love and so the enemy of these women is more often than not internal. Perhaps, the self-hatred and inner fragmentation of these protagonists condones the violators' molestation as something masochistic self-laceration as a necessary rite.

This study has also shown that the novels of Jhabvala are always haunted with the over-possessive and hypnotising masculine rapacity in the garb of religiosity of this continent of spiritual heritage. The novelist has sarcastically attacked the new rising guru-cults in India spreading all over the world. In this case, she appears to be prejudiced against this sub-continent because she has almost generalised the portrayal of spiritual mentors as criminal, deceptive and rapacious exploiters of westerners. In presenting the predicament of western women in India, Jhabvala has portrayed their innocent commitments to the spiritual healers who are nothing more than the fraudulent womanisers in the garb of spirituality. This fraud has also crossed the borders and in the American phase it has become more enigmatic due to racial admixture and also more nightmarish in its consequences. The purpose of feminine self-realisation is, time and again, frustrated and crushed by these rogues in their false promises to bring spiritual rejuvenation to the naive protagonists. The over-possessive Oriental chauvinism and essentially tragic vulnerability of western women and even men with femininity in their nature, are picturised with a sympathetic attitude towards the westerners and a general condemnation of the Indian spiritualism. If this be the personal assessment of Jhabvala regarding spiritual heritage of this land of old renown, then it is only an unqualified impression of her European sensibility.

In the novels of the Indian phase parents are over possessive and so harmful to the righteous growth of their children. In Indo-European phase parents are absolutely absent as young protagonists have renounced their European relations to enter in illusionary intimacy with Indians. In the third phase, the dissolution of anchoring socio-cultural institutions in the western world after the holocaust has been presented with all its serious ramifications. As the very basic structure of socio-cultural institutions has collapsed, the generations are suffering from emotional aridity, alienation, and self-hatred and the deprived children are becoming easy victims of the fraudulent mechanism having the semblance of new family groups. Jhabvala vehemently attacks the selfishness and carelessness of modern parents who are responsible for the internal disintegration and sexual hazards of their deprived children. The novelist also hints that grandparents have comparatively closer relations with the new younger generation rather than parents and this distance from parents is responsible for their predicament of self-hatred, psychic disorders and nymphomaniac passions.

A rigorous survey of the novels of Ruth Prawer Jhabvala explicates the predicament of the feminine sensibility in her fictional world and it appears imperative to re-define womanhood in this world of mysteriously enigmatic submission of woman to male powers. To say that for all her best efforts the visionary creative artist, Ruth Jhabvala has not been able to create a role-model of womanhood free of dependence syndrome, bears eloquent testimony to the age-old belief posited in a well-known adage: 'The character in action of woman or the destiny of man is not known to God even: man as such can never know it.[1] Man is mostly governed by head and is an understandable phenomenon but woman is governed by heart that is most inscrutable part of God's creation. Also woman is said to be the last creation of God and is a mystery and an unanswered and unanswerable puzzle of this human world. This is, however, not to belittle Jhabvala who has in her own way accepted the challenge and paved many untrodden paths into human psyche—especially of woman. Being a creation of a particular ambience, Jhabvala has her limitations, too. She has not been able to sketch the traditional ideal woman of India, who is almost synonymous with *Sati*, *Pativratah* and *Grahlakshmi*. Perhaps, Jhabvala could not find the woman of this character in the middle-class society portrayed in her novels and this shows how the elite class in India, as elsewhere, is after glamour even at the cost of spiritual grace.

But Jhabvala has evolved her well-acknowledged and practical notion of womanhood. Woman can become a complete identity in modern sense of the word only when the derogatory notion about her sex is fully eradicated from her own psychological perceptions as well as from the mind of man. It is equally clear that the predicament of woman's exploitation can never be eradicated whatsoever power or freedom is assigned to her till woman remains isolated in her struggle for self-identity. The self-actualisation of woman will be possible only when womenfolk extend a responsive and supporting hand towards their fellow creatures in this process. The novelist sweeps the whole gamut of feminine feelings and experiences with a commanding hand and from a woman's point of view. Moreover, she treats the female issues with a sense of self-awareness and confidence to give voice to the common agonising cry of women against what man/woman has made of woman. Thus, Jhabvala articulates the powerful elemental passions and every woman vicariously shares the fate of her protagonists and herein lies the beauty of these novels.

In relation to the technical embellishments it is noteworthy that Ruth Jhabvala's artistic vision and craftsmanship have progressively matured and enriched along with the novelist's passage through the successive phases of her literary career. Technically, she initiated her novels with single plot, and flat stories articulating the clash of parents and children on the issues of modernity and emancipation of women. With her entrance into the Indo-European phase Jhabvala introduced not only double but also triple protagonists at a time—Judy, Etta and Clarissa in *A Backward Place*, Lee, Margaret and Evie in *A New Dominion*—with a purpose to give kaleidoscopic exposure to varying degrees of European sensibility of womenfolk. With her most celebrated novel *Heat and Dust* Jhabvala initiated with her most appreciated flashback technique which is a good hint at her screenplay career. The two co-heroines of the novel represent the predicament of expatriate women with a gap of 50 years in pre- and post-independent India. Jhabvala has successfully handled these two plots shining and inter-reflecting each other to give artistic beauty to the novel. With her move to the States Jhabvala's simultaneous career as screenplay writer brought almost equal reputation to the author. Obviously, the screenplay technique is beautifully incorporated in her craftsmanship as a novelist dealing simultaneously with new international dimensions of cosmopolitan people of three or even four generations. The triple protagonists and the masquerade of three and even four generations in flashback are really innovative advancements in the field of novel-writing. In addition to this her mild irony and comic portrayal of the Indian women turned into satire in the second phase of expatriate femininity and finally this has been replaced by acid sarcasm in the portrayal of the self-delusions and disasters of western women in modern times. With the progressive maturity of Jhabvala's vision and skill her focus has probed deep into the feminine soul and psyche of the American protagonists with an artistic excellence. To sum up, it is no exaggeration to state that with these literary embellishments and her superb theme of search for self-definition of woman Jhabvala is certainly, a notch or two above not only the contemporary women novelists but also her predecessors both in India and abroad.

NOTE

1. The popular saying is—*Tiriya charit purusheshya bhagyam devo nnieh janati, huto manushyah.*

Select Bibliography

I. PRIMARY SOURCES

(A) Novels

Jhabvala, Ruth Prawer. *Amrita: To Whom She Will*. London: Penguin Books, 1985. (First Published in 1955)

———. *The Nature of Passion*. London: Penguin Books, 1956. (First Published in 1956)

———. *Esmond in India*. London: Penguin Books, 1980. (First Published in 1957)

———. *The Householder*. Middlesex, London: Penguin Books, 1980. (First Published in 1960)

———. *Get Ready for Battle*. Middlesex, London: Penguin Books, 1981. (First Published in 1962)

———. *A Backward Place*. Delhi: Hind Pocket Books, 1965. (First Published in 1965)

———. *A New Dominion*. London: Granada Publishing Ltd., 1972. (First Published in 1972)

———. *Heat and Dust*. London: Futura Publications, Macdonald & Co. Publishers Ltd., 1976. (First Published in 1975)

———. *In Search of Love and Beauty*. Middlesex, London: Penguin Books, 1986. (First Published in 1983)

———. *Three Continents*. London: Penguin Books, 1988. (First Published in 1987)

———. *Poet and Dancer*. London: Penguin Books, 1994. (First Published in 1993)

———. *Shards of Memory*. London: Penguin Books, 1996. (First Published in 1995)

(B) Short Stories (Collections)

Jhabvala, Ruth Prawer. *Like Birds, Like Fishes*. London: John Murrey, 1963

———. *A Stronger Climate*. London: John Murrey, 1968.

———. *An Experience of India*. New York: Morton, 1972.

———. *How I Became a Holy Mother and Other Stories*. New York: Penguin Books Ltd., 1976.

———. *East into Upper East: Plain Tales From, New York and New Delhi*. London: John Murrey, 1998.

(C) Miscellaneous Writings

Jhabvala, Ruth Prawer. "Moonlight, Jasmine and Rickets", *The New York Times*. New York, April 22, 1975, p. 35.

———. "Neither Love nor Loathing for India", *The Hindustan Times* (Sunday Magazine), Delhi, July 27, 1980, p. 1.

———. "Disinheritance", *Blackwood's Edinburgh Magazine*. July 1979, pp. 7-8.

———. *Autobiography of a Princess*, New York: Harper and Row, 1975.

———. Ruth Prawer Jhabvala's Letter quoted in *Contemporary Novelists*. New York: St. Martin's Press, 1976, p. 270.

II. SECONDARY SOURCES

Agarwal, Ramlal. *Ruth Prawer Jhabvala: A Study of Her Fiction*. New Delhi: Sterling Publishers Pvt. Ltd., 1991.

———. *Heat and Dust* (Book Review), Quest, 99, Ranchi, Jan-Feb. 1976, pp. 87-90.

Alladi, Uma. *Woman and Her Family*. New Delhi: Sterling Publishers Pvt. Ltd., 1989.

Banerjee, Jaya. *The Vintage Book of Feminism* (Book Review), *The Essential Writings of the Contemporary Women's*

Movement, ed. Miriam Schneir Vintage. New Delhi: Rupa and Co. 1995, p. 13.

Bhatnagar, K.G. *Realism in Major Indo-English Fiction.* Bareilly: Prakash Book Depot, 1980.

Beals. *Culture in Process.* London: University Press, 1967, p. 85.

Belliappa, Meena. *A Study of Jhabvala's Fiction.* Miscellany, 43 (1971), p. 37.

Coward, Rosalind. "The Novel Changes Women's Lives: Are Women's Novels Feminist Novels", *Feminist Review* 5, 1980.

Crane, Ralph J. "A Forsterian Connection: Ruth Prawer Jhabvala and A Passage to India", *Passages to Ruth Prawer Jhabvala.* New Delhi: Sterling Publishers Pvt. Ltd., 1991, pp. 50-63.

Dass, Kamala. *Summer in Calcutta*, New Delhi: Everest Press, 1965, p. 52.

de Beauvoir, Simon. *The Second Sex,* trans., by H.M. Parshley. London: Penguin Books, 1983.

De, Shobha. "Sex in the Time of Stress in Khushwant Singh and Shobha De: Uncertain Liaisons", *Sex, Strife and Togetherness in Urban India.* Delhi: Viking/Penguin India, 1993.

Dhawan, R.K. *Explorations in Modern Indo-English Fiction.* New Delhi: Bahri Publications Pvt. Ltd., 1982.

Dwivedi, A.N. "A Feminist Voice: Judith Write", *Points of View* (Feminism Special Number), Vol. II, No. 2, Winter, 1995, pp. 80-89.

Gilman, Sander L. *Jewish Self-Hatred: Anti-Semitism and the Hidden Language of the Jews.* The John Hopkins University Press, 1986.

Goonaratne, Yasmine. *Silence, Exile and Cunning: The Fiction of Ruth Prawer Jhabvala*, Hyderabad: Orient Longman Ltd., 1983.

———. "Apollo, Krishna, Superman: The Image of India in Ruth Prawer Jhabvala's Ninth Novel", *Ariel*, 15, No. 2, 1984, pp. 109-17.

———. *Ruth Jhabvala's Screen Plays: Passages to Ruth Prawer Jhabvala*, ed. Ralph J. Crane. New Delhi: Sterling Publishers Pvt. Ltd., 1991, pp. 104-09.

Gray John. *Men are from Mars: Women are from Venus*. India, HarperCollins Publishers Third Impression, 1997.

Guerin, Wilfred L. Labor, Morgan, *A Handbook of Critical Approaches to Literature*, IVth edition. New York and Oxford: Oxford University Press, 1998.

Gupta, Neeta. *Knocks of Modernity in Jhabvala's Novels: Women in Indo-Anglian Fiction*, ed. Naresh K. Jain. New Delhi: Manohar Publishers and Distributors, 1998, pp. 56-74.

Hutcheon, Linda. *A Poetics of Post-Modernism*. New York and London: Routledge, 1988.

Iyengar, K.R. Srinivasa. *Indian Writing in English*. New Delhi: Sterling Publishers Pvt. Ltd., 1985.

Jain, Naresh K. *Tradition, Modernity and Change: Women in Indo-Anglian Fiction*. New Delhi: Manohar Publishers and Distributors, 1998.

Jussawala, Feroza. "On Three Continents: The Inside, the Outside", *Passages to Ruth Prawer Jhabvala*, ed. Ralph J. Crane. New Delhi: Sterling Publishers Pvt. Ltd., 1991, pp. 87-94.

Krishnaswamy, Shanta. *The Woman in Indian Fiction in English*. New Delhi: Ashish Publishing House, 1983.

———. *Ruth Prawer Jhabvala: White Woman's Burden, Glimpses of Women in India*. New Delhi: Ashish Publishing House, 1984, pp. 281-337.

Leon and Grinberg. *Psycho-analytical Perspectives on Migration and Exile*, trans. Maney Festinger New Haven: Yale University Press, 1988.

Livett, Jennifer. "Propinquity and Distance: The American Novels of Jhabvala and Bellow", *Passages to Ruth Prawer*

Jhabvala, ed. Ralph J. Crane. New Delhi: Sterling Publishers Pvt. Ltd., 1991, pp. 63-78.

May, Yolantana. *Conversation with Jhabvala: The New Review*. December 1975, p. 56.

Mehta, Purnima. "The Feminine Image in the Indo-Anglian Novel of the Post Independence Era", *Contemporary Indian Fiction in English*, ed. Avadhesh K. Singh. New Delhi: Creative Books, 1993, pp. 143-47.

Moorehead, Caroline. "A Solitary Writer's Window on the Heat and Dust of India", *The Times*, New York, 20 November 1975, p. 16.

Mukherjee, Meenakshi. "The Ruthless Jhabvala Touch: Review of How I became a Holy Mother", *The Times of India*. 12 September 1976, p. 10.

———. "Journey's End for Jhabvala", *Explorations in Modern Indo-English Fiction*, ed. R.K. Dhawan. New Delhi: Bahri Publications Pvt. Ltd., 1982, pp. 208-13.

———. *The Twice-Born Fiction: Themes and Techniques of the Indian Novel in English*. New Delhi: Amold-Heinmann, 1971.

Nahal, Chaman. "Feminism in English Fiction: Forms and Variations", *Feminism and Recent Fiction in English*, ed. Sushila Singh. New Delhi: Prestige Books, 1991, pp. 14-21.

Naik, M.K. *Aspects of Indian Writing in English*. New Delhi: The Macmillan Press Co., 1979.

———. *A History of Indian English Literature*. New Delhi: Sahitya Academy, 1982.

Pathak, R.S. "Feminist Concerns in Shobha De's Snapshots", *Points of View* (Feminism Special Number), Vol. II, No. 2, Winter, 1995, pp. 90-105.

Pritchett, V.S. "Snares and Delusions", *New Yorker*, 16th June 1973, p. 106.

Rosenberg, Harold. *Discovering the Present: Three Decades in Art, Culture and Politics*, University of Chicago Press, 1973.

Rubin, David. "Ruth Jhabvala in India", *Modern Fiction Studies*, Vol. 50, No. 4. West Lafayette: Perdue Univ. Winter, 1984, pp. 669-85.

Rushdie, Salman. *The Indian Writers in England in Eye of the Beholder: Indian Writing in English*, ed. Maggie Butcher. London: Commonwealth Institute, 1985, p. 75.

Saha, Subhash C. "The Feminist Quest for Truth in Kamala Das's Poems", *Points of View* (Feminism Special Number) Vol. II, No. 2, Winter 1995, pp. 106-12.

Saros, C. and Shahane, V.A. *Modern Fiction Studies*. New Delhi: Vikas Publishing House Pvt. Ltd., 1965.

Saxena, O.P. *Glimpses of Indo-English Fiction*, Vol. 11. New Delhi: Jainsons Publications, 1985.

Shahane, Vasant A. *Ruth Prawer Jhabvala*. New Delhi: Arnold Heinmann Publishers Pvt. Ltd., 1976.

———. "An Artist's Experience of India: Jhabv's Fiction", *Commonwealth Fiction*, ed. R.K. Dhawan. New Delhi: Classical Publishing Company, 1988, pp. 228-44.

Sharma, Arvind. *Sati: Historical and Phenomenological Essays*. Delhi: Motilal Banarasidas, 1988, pp. 77-83.

Sharma, Kavita A. "Jhabvala on God Man", *The Radical Humanist*, Vol. 43, No. 8, Nov. 1979, pp. 32-34.

Sharrad, Paul. "Passing Moments: Irony, Ambivalence and Time in a Backward Place", *Passages to Ruth Prawer Jhabvala*, ed. Ralph J. Crane. New Delhi: Sterling Publishers Pvt. Ltd., 1991.

Shepherd, Ronald. "Yes, Something is Wrong: Obscure Irritants in Ruth Prawer Jhabvala's Short Stories", *Passage to Ruth Prawer Jhabvala*, ed. Ralph J. Crane. New Delhi: Sterling Publishers Pvt. Ltd., 1991, pp. 95-102.

Singer, Milton. *Jhabvala in India: The Jewish Connection*. Delhi: Chanakya Publication, 1994.

———. "Passage to More than India", *When a Great Tradition Modernizes*. New Delhi: Vikas Publishing House, Pvt. Ltd., 1972.

Singh, Khushwant. "India, The Literary Scene", *International Literary Annual*, III. London, 1961, p. 174.

Singh, R.S. *Ironic Vision of a Social Realist: Indian Novel in English*. New Delhi: Arnold Heinmann, 1977, pp. 149-63.

Singh, Sushila. "Outlining Feminist Literary Criticism: Woman as Reader/Writer Perspective", *Points of View*, Vol. II, No. 2, Winter 1995, pp. 1-9.

Singh, T.N. "Feminism and Fiction: Some Reflections", *Feminism and Recent Fiction in English*, ed. Sushila Singh. New Delhi: Prestige Books, 1991, pp. 11-13.

Sinha, K.N. "India, The Literary Scene", *International Literary Annual*, III. London, 1961, p. 174.

Sinha, Shakuntala. "Some Aspects of Intercultural and Interracial interaction in the Novels of Kamala Markandaya and R.P. Jhabvala", *Indian Writings in English*, ed. M.K. Bhatnagar. New Delhi: Atlantic Publishers and Distributors, 1998, pp. 160-66.

Shirwedkar, Meena. *Image of Woman in the Indo-Anglican Novels*. New Delhi: Sterling Publishers Pvt. Ltd., 1979.

Steinworth, Klaus. "The Indo-English Novel", *The Impact of the West on Literature in a Developing Country*, Weisbaden: Fr. Stainer Verlog., 1975.

Sucher, Lourie. *The Fiction of Ruth Prawer Jhabvala: The Politics of Passion*. London: The Macmillan Press Ltd., 1989.

Summerfield, Henry. "Religion Becomes Politics: Ruth Prawer Jhabvala's Tenth Novel", *Passages to Ruth Prawer Jhabvala*, ed. Ralph J. Crane. New Delhi: Sterling Publishers Pvt. Ltd., 1991, pp. 79-86.

Tennyson, Alfred. *The Princess* (1847); *The Works of Lord Alfred Tennyson*, II. London: Macmillan & Co., 1984, p. 78.

Tripathi, J.P. "The Feminist Upsurge in Jaya's Ego in Shashi Deshpande's *That Long Silence*", *Points of View* (Feminism Special Number) Vol. II, No. 2, Winter, 1995, pp. 80-89.

Verghese, C. Paul. *Problems of the Indian Creative Writers in English*. Bombay: Somaiya Publications, 1971.

———. "A Note on Esmond in India", *Journal of India Writing in English*. New Delhi, July 1976, pp. 33-37.

Walsh, William. *Readings in Commonwealth Literature*. London: Oxford University Press, 1973.

Warley, Linda. "The Cuckoo's Nest: The House and Home in Two Early Novels by Ruth Prawer Jhabvala", *Passages to Ruth Prawer Jhabvala*, ed. Ralph J. Crane. New Delhi: Sterling Publishers Pvt. Ltd., 1991, pp. 15-27.

Williams, Hayden Moore. "A Retrospective Look at Ruth Prawer Jhabvala's Career as a Novelist: The Indian Novels", *Passages to Ruth Prawer Jhabvala*, ed. Ralph J. Crane. New Delhi: Sterling Publishers Pvt. Ltd., 1991, pp. 1-14.

———. "Mad Seekers, Doomed Lovers and Cemeteries in India: Jhabvala's *Heat and Dust* and *A New Dominion*", *Commonwealth Fiction*, ed. R.K. Dhawan. New Delhi: Classical Publishing Company, 1998, pp. 253-67.

———. *Studies in Modern Indian Fiction* (Two Volumes). Calcutta: Writers Workshop, 1973.